PRAISE WITH UNDERSTANDING

David and Jill Wright

PATERNOSTER PRESS

EXETER
THE PATERNOSTER PRESS

AUSTRALIA:
Bookhouse Australia Ltd.,
P.O. Box 115, Flemington Markets, NSW 2129

SOUTH AFRICA:
Oxford University Press,
P.O. Box 1141, Cape Town

British Library Cataloguing in Publication Data

Wright, David R.
  Praise with understanding.
  1. Hymns—History and criticism
  I. Title   II. Wright, Jill
  264'.2   BV310

ISBN 0-85364-355-5

Typeset by Busby's Typesetting, 200–201 High Street, Exeter
and Printed in Great Britain for The Paternoster Press,
Paternoster House, 3 Mount Radford Crescent, Exeter, Devon
by The Pitman Press, Bath

Contents

*To Rachel
and Steven*

PREFACE

"Sing praises unto God . . . sing ye with understanding"
(Psalm 47:6 & 7)

T he purpose of this book is to encourage the reading of hymns and the study of hymns: to unlock the hymn book, and to discover meanings.

Many hymns were written to make worship more meaningful and more comprehensible, yet they are in danger of becoming as incomprehensible as some other forms of worship. Although hymns are as widely used and as widely loved as ever, they are thought about much less often than they are sung.

The work has been a joy to undertake. In particular, the quest for the biblical source of inspiration of the authors has proved particularly rewarding. Very often, the source is the Psalms: the greatest hymn book is an inspiration for all other hymn books. But there are references to all parts of the Bible in these thirty hymns, from Genesis to Revelation, and even to the Book of Tobit in the Apocrypha. Quotations are from the Authorised Version of the Bible, because this was the version used by the authors or translators.

The authors of these hymns are separated by as much as 1500 years; their homes, too, are separated by 1500 miles and more. They come from a wide variety of Christian backgrounds—Roman Catholic, Orthodox, Anglican and Free Church, yet the hymns appeal to Christians of all traditions. We hope that the exposition, too, will similarly be found to be widely acceptable, and labelled as "Christian", with no other adjective. Hundreds of other hymns are equally worthy of inclusion; we have deliberately included a few less well-known hymns to illustrate the great variety of excellent hymns that can be used in worship. In this volume, hymns from this century have been excluded.

There are other books about hymns, but most are out of print—an indication of the neglect of the study of hymns. The majority of books about hymns offer stories loosely linked to hymns, or, at the other extreme, are reference books listing the origins and amendments of hymns, sometimes dubbed "Refs. for Revs.". This book seeks to follow the tradition of Christian scholarship that tries to put into practice the words of the Apostle Paul: "I will sing with the Spirit, and I will sing with the understanding also" *(1 Corinthians 14:15)*.*

David and Jill Wright, Mulbarton, Norfolk

* Scripture references are shown thus. Verse and line references in hymns appear thus (2.1).

A SAFE STRONGHOLD OUR GOD IS STILL
Martin Luther (1483–1546)

"God is our refuge and strength: a very present help in trouble"
(Psalm 46:1)

1 A safe stronghold our God is still,
   A trusty shield and weapon;
He'll help us clear from all the ill
That hath us now o'ertaken.
   The ancient prince of hell
   Hath risen with purpose fell;
   Strong mail of craft and power
   He weareth in this hour;
On earth is not his fellow.

2 With force of arms we nothing can,
   Full soon were we down-ridden;
But for us fights the proper Man,
Whom God himself hath bidden.
   Ask ye, Who is this same?
   Christ Jesus is his name,
   The Lord Sabaoth's Son;
   He, and no other one,
Shall conquer in the battle.

3 And were this world all devils o'er,
   And watching to devour us,
We lay it not to heart so sore;
Not they can overpower us.
   And let the prince of ill
   Look grim as e'er he will,
   He harms us not a whit;
   For why? his doom is writ;
A word shall quickly slay him.

4 God's word, for all their craft and force,
   One moment shall not linger,
But, spite of hell, shall have its course;
'Tis written by His finger.
   And though they take our life,
   Goods, honour, children, wife,
   Yet is their profit small;
   These things shall vanish all,
The city of God remaineth.

Martin Luther was the key figure in the Reformation in Germany. He was born in 1483, the son of a miner in Eisleben. After graduating from the University of Erfurt, he entered the Augustinian Convent there, and became a priest of the Roman Catholic Church in 1507. His struggles against corruption in the Church led to his famous notice on the church door at Wittenberg in 1517. After his burning of the "Papal Bull" in 1520, and his refusal to retract his doctrines at the Diet of Worms, he went into hiding for a year. From 1522 he was the leader of the Reformation.

As well as translating the Bible, Luther wrote 37 hymns. He wrote, "It is my plan to make psalms in the vernacular, for the people, and that the words may all be exceedingly simple and common, such as plain folk may understand, yet withall pure and skillfully translated." This hymn is thus older than any originally written in English that are still in use today.

The translation is a 19th-century one by Thomas Carlyle, first published in 1831 in Fraser's Magazine. Another well-known translation is "A mighty fortress is our God; a bulwark never failing" by an American, F. H. Hedge (1805–1890). The hymn has been translated into over 50 languages. The tune is inseparable from the hymn—it is also the theme of the final movement of Mendelssohn's "Reformation" Symphony. Although the hymn has been called "the Marseillaise of the Reformation", the theology in it is now as acceptable to Roman Catholics as to Protestants.

L uther starts this great hymn with a rendering of the first verse of Psalm 46. But this is not a paraphrase of the psalm: the words incorporate ideas from both Old and New Testaments.

The conflict of good and evil is identified clearly in verse 1. Doubtless originally the hymn was seen as a means of denouncing evil within the Church, but the message is much wider. The power of evil in the world is pictured vividly, both in the first verse, and in the last (v. 4.5–6). The picture of destruction is as complete as in the Book of Job. Against this evil, "force of arms" (v.2.1) is totally useless. BUT—the key word in verse 2.3—"if God be for us, who can be against us?" (*Romans 8:31* and verse 2 of hymn). The phrase in verse 3.9, "A word shall quickly slay him", sounds obscure, but is explained in the first 4 lines of verse 4. The reference may be to "The sword of the Spirit, which is the Word of God" (*Ephesians 6:17*) or to "the word of God is quick, and powerful, and sharper than any two-edged sword . . ." (*Hebrews 4:12*). The power of the word of God is the only worthwhile weapon, repelling the attacks of all the forces of evil. Similarly, when he was tempted, it was with the word of God that Jesus silenced Satan (*Luke 4*).

The other translation of this hymn, by F. H. Hedge, also offers helpful contrasts between fear and trust:

"We will not fear; for God hath willed
His truth to triumph through us."

and between physical death and the triumph of truth:

"The body they may kill:
God's truth abideth still.
His kingdom is for ever."

As PANTS THE HART FOR COOLING STREAMS
Nahum Tate (1652–1715)
and Nicholas Brady (1659–1726)

"Like as the hart desireth the waterbrooks,
So longeth my soul after thee, O God"
(Psalm 42:1)

---

1 As pants the hart for cooling streams
    When heated in the chase,
So longs my soul, O God, for thee,
    And thy refreshing grace.

2 For thee, my God, the living God,
    My thirsty soul doth pine:
O when shall I behold thy face,
    Thou Majesty Divine!

3 Why restless, why cast down, my soul?
    Hope still, and thou shalt sing
The praise of him who is thy God,
    Thy health's eternal spring.

4 To Father, Son, and Holy Ghost,
    The God whom we adore,
Be glory, as it was, is now,
    And shall be evermore.

Nahum Tate (1652–1715) and Nicholas Brady (1659–1726) were both Irish Anglicans. Tate became Poet Laureate in 1690; his writings were mainly for the stage. Brady was ordained, and served in churches in London, Richmond (Surrey), Clapham (London), and Stratford-upon-Avon.

In 1696 they produced the "New Version" of the Psalms: metrical hymns based closely on the words of the Authorised Version. Most have long since ceased to be used, except in Scotland, but one other is the well-known hymn, "Through all the changing scenes of life" (Psalm 34). They also paraphrased certain other passages of Scripture, the best known by far being "While shepherds watched their flocks by night" (Luke 2:8–15).

Only a small proportion of this paraphrase is now sung; originally it had 48 lines. The first two verses of the hymn are only the first two verses of an eleven-verse Psalm. The initial verse loses some of its force in a cool and moist country: one needs to imagine the mountainous land of Israel, and its intense heat and aridity. Streams are few and far between in that country. In such circumstances, the longing for water must be overwhelming, while the realisation that water is distant and hard to find must be worrying and depressing. The psalmist is speaking to God, even though God seems as distant, and as totally out-of-sight to him, as "cooling streams" were to the hart (a deer).

Perhaps the most important part of this hymn is that it offers no easy or short-term solution to the problem of depression. Verse 3 of the hymn is based on verse 5 of the psalm, which is repeated at the end of both *Psalm 42* and *Psalm 43*. There is indeed hope—but hope is for the future. The recognition that King David, and countless others, have experienced darkness and distance from God in their lives, can be in itself a great encouragement to everyone. The hymn concludes by naming God "the eternal spring"—this is not a phrase from the psalm, but it is an excellent conclusion for us to reflect upon. We thirst for God (v.2); and he is a never-failing spring of water. In his depression, the Psalmist still has the recollection of worship and fellowship, which supports his hope and trust in God. The "Doxology" (v.4) is, of course, a Christian addition to the Psalm.

AT THE NAME OF JESUS
Caroline Maria Noel (1817–1877)

"At the name of Jesus, every knee should bow"
(Philippians 2:10)

1 At the Name of Jesus
  Every knee shall bow,
Every tongue confess Him
  King of glory now.
'Tis the Father's pleasure
  We should call Him Lord,
Who from the beginning
  Was the mighty Word:

2 Mighty and mysterious
  In the highest height,
God from everlasting,
  Very Light of Light:
In the Father's bosom
  With the Spirit blest,
Love, in Love eternal,
  Rest, in perfect Rest.

3 At His voice creation
  Sprang at once to sight,
All the angel faces,
  All the hosts of light,
Thrones and dominations,
  Stars upon their way,
All the heavenly orders
  In their great array.

4 Humbled for a season,
  To receive a Name
From the lips of sinners
  Unto whom He came,
Faithfully he bore it,
  Spotless to the last,
Brought it back victorious
  When from death he passed:

5 Bore it up triumphant
  With its human light,
Through all ranks of creatures,
  To the central height,
To the throne of Godhead,
  To the Father's breast;
Filled it with the glory
  Of that perfect rest.

6 Name him, brothers, name him,
  With love as strong as death,
But with awe and wonder,
  And with bated breath;
He is God the Saviour,
  He is Christ the Lord,
Ever to be worshipped,
  Trusted, and adored.

7 In your hearts enthrone him;
  There let him subdue
All that is not holy,
  All that is not true:
Crown him as your captain
  In temptation's hour;
Let his will enfold you
  In its light and power.

8 Brothers, this Lord Jesus
  Shall return again,
With his Father's glory,
  With his Angel train;
For all wreaths of empire
  Meet upon his brow,
And our hearts confess him
  King of glory now.

The author, Caroline Maria Noel, lived from 1817 to 1877. She was the daughter of the Rev. and Hon. Gerard Noel, vicar of Romsey, Hampshire. She experienced much illness, and identified with other sufferers, even to the extent of publishing a book in 1861 called "The Name of Jesus, and other verses for the sick and lonely". This hymn is the only one of her compositions in widespread use today, perhaps because it avoids being introspective.

"At the Name of Jesus" comes from mid-Victorian times, yet the modern tune by Geoffrey Beaumont has made it one of the most popular hymns with children and adults. It is a hymn that has a simple theme, yet it is explored in more depth and detail than many other popular hymns. The basis of the hymn is Paul's Epistle to the Philippians 2:5–11.

It starts in the future: *every knee shall* bow to Jesus (v.1.2); it moves rapidly to the present tense: Jesus is the King of Glory *now* (v.1.4), and then goes into the furthest past: Jesus, from the beginning— from Creation—was the mighty Word (v.1.8) (*John 1:1*).

Verse 4 refers to Jesus' earthly ministry—he came to receive the Name (v.4.2) of "Saviour" from the sinners for whom he came. This name was borne faithfully, to his death and resurrection. Then (v.5.1) in the Ascension, he carried that name to Heaven.

Verse 6 turns to our response—we are to name him, reverently, for he is Lord as well as Saviour. Therefore, we need to make him King of our heart. His will is to become ours (v.7.7).

Verse 8 moves again to the future: "Brothers, this Lord Jesus Shall return again". Some hymn books have altered this to the present tense: "Brothers, this Lord Jesus/Dwells with us again". Finally, all versions invite us to "confess Him, King of Glory now" (v.8.8).

CHRIST IS OUR CORNER-STONE
John Chandler (1806–1876)

(We are) "of the household of God, and are built upon the foundation of the apostles and prophets, Jesus Christ himself being the chief corner stone; in whom all the building fitly framed together groweth unto an holy temple in the Lord; in whom ye also are builded together for an habitation of God through the Spirit."

(Ephesians 2:19–22)

1 Christ is our corner-stone,
   On him alone we build;
With his true saints alone
   The courts of heaven are filled;
On his great love Our hopes we place
Of present grace And joys above.

2 O! then with hymns of praise
   These hallowed courts shall ring;
Our voices we will raise
   The Three in One to sing;
And thus proclaim In joyful song,
Both loud and long, That glorious Name.

3 Here, gracious God, do thou
   For evermore draw nigh;
Accept each faithful vow,
   And mark each suppliant sigh;
In copious shower On all who pray
Each holy day Thy blessings pour.

4 Here may we gain from heaven
   The grace which we implore:
And may that grace, once given,
   Be with us evermore;
Until that day, When all the blest
To endless rest Are called away.

'Urbs beata Hierusalem,' is a long and ancient hymn, probably written in the 6th or 7th century. John Julian describes it as "simple, striking, and devotional". Archbishop Trench called it "a rugged but fine old hymn". The hymn as printed here is in fact only the second part of the original. The first part, in Chandler's version, is no longer used, but it is still familiar in J. M. Neale's translation: "Blessed city, heavenly Salem". Verse 5 of Neale's hymn can be recognised as coming from the same source as Chandler's hymn:
"Christ is made the sure foundation;
Christ, the head and corner-stone."

John Chandler, the translator of the version printed here, was born at Witley, a village near Godalming in Surrey. He became vicar of Witley in 1837 in succession to his father, after having studied at Corpus Christi College, Oxford. He was one of several 19th-century translators of ancient hymns, and he published "Hymns of the Primitive Church" in the year he became vicar of Witley. He lived to be 70 years old.

"Christ is our corner-stone"! This must be one of the finest, and most memorable, first lines of any hymn. The image does not fit modern structures of concrete and steel, but there are enough old buildings in every town for the importance of corner-stones still to be recognised. The term "corner-stone" is found both in the Old Testament and in the New Testament, but it is clearly the passage from Ephesians (opposite) that is the basis of the hymn. The essence of the church is the people, not the building: this is well expressed both in the passage in Ephesians and in the hymn, but it remains an elusive concept to those who only see church buildings from the outside.

The basis of all our hope is "his great love" (v.1.5). The key to both our present and our future lies in that phrase. The book of Revelation frequently pictures "the courts of heaven" filled with "his true saints" (v.1.3–4) who continually sing God's praise (v.2.1). In verse 2, the author links the praises of God's saints below with those above. Thus the hymn turns naturally to praise the name of God, the "three in one" (v.2.4). The passage from Ephesians (opposite) concludes with a clear reference to the Trinity (*Ephesians 2:22*): "In whom (Christ) ye also are builded together for an habitation of God through the Spirit".

The beginning of verse 3 suggests a special occasion. Some hymn books place the hymn in a section for "Dedication Festivals", but it is also an ideal hymn for a wedding service, with the confident first verse and the prayer in the third verse. But "each holy day" can refer not just to special days, but to every Sunday, and indeed to every weekday too. Thus we pray that God will accept our vows and prayers, and that he will bless us (v.3.1–4).

In the final verse we ask for his grace now and always: the "hope of grace" (v.1.6–7) has become the confident prayer (v.3.1–4). The hymn thus returns to its first theme, with a new confidence that is based on the answer to the prayer of verse 3.

13

COME, HOLY GHOST, OUR SOULS INSPIRE

"The love of God is shed abroad in our hearts
by the Holy Ghost"
(*Romans 5:5*)

1 Come, Holy Ghost, our souls inspire,
And lighten with celestial fire;
Thou the anointing Spirit art,
Who dost thy sevenfold gifts impart:

2 Thy blessèd unction from above
Is comfort, life, and fire of love;
Enable with perpetual light
The dullness of our blinded sight:

3 Anoint and cheer our soilèd face
With the abundance of thy grace:
Keep far our foes, give peace at home;
Where thou art guide no ill can come.

4 Teach us to know the Father, Son,
And thee, of Both, to be but One;
That through the ages all along
This may be our endless song,
Praise to thy eternal merit,
Father, Son, and Holy Spirit.   Amen.

This is the only hymn printed in the Prayer Book of the Church of England, but its origin is much older than that. It is a translation of a Latin hymn, which was certainly written before the 10th century. The author is uncertain, but may be Rhabanus Maurus, Archbishop of Mainz (*c.* 776–856). This hymn is thus a reminder that hymn-singing is a very old Christian tradition. Watts and Wesley revived a tradition, rather than creating a new style of worship.

The translation here is by J. Cosin, and was first published in 1627 in his "Collection of Private Devotions in the Practice of the Ancient Church". Cosin was born in Norwich in 1594, and became Master of a Cambridge college; he later became Bishop of Durham. Other translations of the hymn are also in use: John Dryden's "Creator Spirit, by whose aid" and Robert Bridges' "Come, O Creator Spirit, come".

I n the context of the Church of England Prayer Book this hymn is sung during ordination services, but in other churches it is most often sung at Whitsun. Each verse is a prayer to the Holy Spirit. First of all, the prayer is for inspiration and light. The idea of celestial fire giving light (v.1.2) is a reference to the coming of the Holy Spirit at Pentecost (*Acts 2:3*): "There appeared unto them cloven tongues like as of fire, and it sat upon each of them. And they were all filled with the Holy Spirit."

The prayer for inspiration, light and fire leads on to the "sevenfold gifts" of the Spirit (v.1.4). Paul wrote to the Corinthians about practical gifts given by the Spirit for building up the Church (*1 Corinthians 12*), and he wrote to the Galatians about the "fruit of the Spirit" in individual Christian lives: "love, joy, peace, longsuffering, gentleness, goodness, faith, meekness and temperance" (*Galatians 5:22*). Of these, love (expounded in *1 Corinthians 13*) is specifically mentioned in this hymn (v.2.2)—but the hymn invites reflection on all the gifts and fruits of the Spirit.

The prayer in verse 2 is for light—a constant theme in the Bible. It also speaks of comfort: the title "the Comforter" is used by Jesus for the Holy Spirit (e.g. *John 14:16*), and in modern meaning the title is closer to "the Strengthener".

The prayer moves on to safety at home, and confidently states: "Where Thou art Guide no ill can come" (v.3.4). The final verse is a doxology, but it is more than that: it is a prayer for *knowledge*, which comes from both teaching and personal experience. And the aim is not academic satisfaction but endless praise to God the Trinity.

FIGHT THE GOOD FIGHT
WITH ALL THY MIGHT
John Samuel Bewley Monsell (1811–1875)

"Fight the good fight of faith;
lay hold on eternal life"
(*1 Timothy 6:12*)

1 Fight the good fight with all thy might;
   Christ is thy strength, and Christ thy right:
   Lay hold on life, and it shall be
   Thy joy and crown eternally.

2 Run the straight race through God's
        good grace,
   Lift up thine eyes, and seek His face;
   Life with its way before thee lies;
   Christ is the path, and Christ the prize.

3 Cast care aside; upon thy Guide
   Lean, and His mercy will provide;
   Lean, and the trusting soul shall prove
   Christ is its life, and Christ its love.

4 Faint not, nor fear, His arm is near;
   He changeth not, and thou art dear;
   Only believe, and thou shalt see
   That Christ is all in all to thee.

Today we sing only half of the original hymn, which was first published as five verses, each of six lines. The author was the son of the Archdeacon of Londonderry (Church of Ireland), and became a clergyman in Ireland. In 1853 he moved to Surrey, becoming vicar of Egham, then rector of St. Nicholas, Guildford. He wrote nearly 300 hymns, and much poetry as well. He stated that he wished to make hymns "more fervent and joyous" and less "distant and reserved". Other well-known hymns of his include "O worship the Lord in the beauty of holiness" and "I hunger and I thirst".

Military imagery is no longer popular in Christian worship, yet it would be a pity if "Fight the Good Fight" fell out of use because of its first four words. For this hymn refers to the *good* fight of faith—it is in no way connected with battles or Crusades. And when St. Paul coined the original metaphor (*Ephesians 6:10–17*), it was based on his knowledge of the occupying Roman army, which was unpopular with the local people.

"Christ is thy strength and Christ thy right" (v.1.2), refers not to "might makes right" but to Christ giving his righteousness and strength to his followers. This depends (v.2) on "running the straight race"—another Pauline metaphor which has been overworked, but still offers a clear idea of a single aim. By "seeking his face" (v.2.2) Christ becomes our path towards true life, and the "prize" at the end of the race (v.2.4).

"Cast care aside" (v.3.1) could sound irresponsible, but care in this context means worry. The author was doubtless thinking of *Hebrews 12:1–2*, where runners entered in the race are reminded to leave aside any weight (of sin and worry), and also of *1 Peter 5:7*: "Casting all your care upon him for he careth for you". "His mercy will provide" (v.3.2) may refer to "My grace is sufficient for you" (*2 Corinthians 12:9*) or perhaps to Christ's own words, "Take no thought for the morrow. . . ." (*Matthew 6:34*).

Verse 4 completes this picture of the Christian life. There is no need to faint or to fear—a helpful reassurance after the other exhortations in the hymn, which could seem so discouraging. Ultimately the author reminds us that Christ never changes, that he is always near—and that faith is the key.

17

FROM THEE
ALL SKILL AND SCIENCE FLOW
Charles Kingsley (1819–1875)

"The fear of the Lord is the beginning of wisdom"
(Psalm 111.10)

1 From Thee all skill and science flow;
    All pity, care, and love,
  All calm and courage, faith and hope:
    O pour them from above!

2 And part them, Lord, to each and all
    As each and all shall need,
  To rise like incense, each to Thee,
    In noble thought and deed.

3 And hasten, Lord, that perfect day
    When pain and death shall cease;
  And Thy just rule shall fill the earth
    With health and light and peace;

4 When ever blue the sky shall gleam,
    And ever green the sod;
  And man's rude work deface no more
    The paradise of God.

Charles Kingsley (1819–1875) was the son of the vicar of Holne, Devonshire (and subsequently rector of St. Luke's, Chelsea) and was educated at the Universities of London and Cambridge. He, too, became ordained, and served initially at Eversley, near Reading. His "revolutionary" Socialist ideas led the Bishop of London to prohibit him from preaching within his diocese—but by the age of 40 he became Chaplain to the Queen, and eventually a canon of Chester, and then of Westminster itself. In 1860 he became Professor of Modern History at Cambridge. He is also, of course, a well-known novelist, being author of "The Water Babies" and "Westward Ho!" He had a genuine interest in the welfare of the people, and this hymn was sung at the opening of the New Wing of the Children's Hospital in Birmingham. The original first verse, beginning "Accept this building, gracious Lord" has been forgotten, but verses 3 to 6—the present hymn—retain a full relevance for today.

Relatively few hymns take man's wisdom as their starting point. Charles Kingsley's hymn is an exception. He interprets the well-known verse, "The fear of the Lord is the beginning of wisdom" (*Psalm 111:10* and *Proverbs 9:10*). The resulting first line of this hymn could be inscribed on *every* Christian's desk or workbench—and it is as relevant now as when it was written in the days of the great Victorian scientific inventions. From the Lord comes all wisdom and all the good qualities of life (v.1.1 & 3). Kingsley concludes the verse with a prayer that God will give these gifts liberally to us.

Verse 2 may seem bland at first sight—but it conveys a message almost as revolutionary as the Magnificat ("He has cast down the mighty from their seat, and exalted the humble and meek"). For the second line of this verse is a rendering of the phrase "to each according to his need": a central idea of the Christian Socialists, of which Charles Kingsley was a leader.

Verses 3 and 4 look forward to a better world. It could seem trite, or even pure Victorian overoptimism, but in the context of verse 1 we can indeed ask God to use us to make our God-given skill and science work for health, for light and for peace. Kingsley wrote a century before pollution and the quality of the environment became a major concern—yet verse 4 is every environmentalist's prayer.

GOD MOVES IN A MYSTERIOUS WAY
William Cowper (1731–1800)

"What I do thou knowest not now, but thou shalt know hereafter"
(John 13:7)

1 God moves in a mysterious way
  His wonders to perform;
He plants his footsteps in the sea,
  And rides upon the storm.

2 Deep in unfathomable mines
  Of never-failing skill
He treasures up his bright designs,
  And works his sovereign will.

3 Ye fearful saints, fresh courage take,
  The clouds ye so much dread
Are big with mercy, and shall break
  In blessings on your head.

4 Judge not the Lord by feeble sense,
  But trust him for his grace;
Behind a frowning providence
  He hides a smiling face.

5 His purposes will ripen fast,
  Unfolding every hour;
The bud may have a bitter taste,
  But sweet will be the flower.

6 Blind unbelief is sure to err,
  And scan his work in vain;
God is his own interpreter,
  And he will make it plain.

William Cowper (1731–1800) has been called "the greatest poet of his age". His father was rector of Great Berkhamsted, Herts., and was a chaplain to King George II. William studied at Westminster School, was articled to an attorney, and was called to the Bar when aged 23. However, he had spells of deep depression. He lived in Huntingdon, in Olney, Bucks., and finally in East Dereham, Norfolk. While at Olney, he worked with John Newton on the "Olney Hymns". These hymns were sung not in church—this was before hymns were acceptable in Anglican churches—but at mid-week prayer meetings.

Cowper wrote several fine hymns, including "O for a closer walk with God"; "Hark my soul, it is the Lord"; and "Jesus, where'er thy people meet".

This hymn was originally published anonymously. Six parts of this short hymn are included in the "Oxford Dictionary of Quotations"—more than from any other hymn. The New Testament verse quoted at the top of this page is Cowper's own choice of text for this hymn.

Few well-known poets are also well known as hymn writers, but William Cowper is one exception. Furthermore, few poets find the short lines of the "Common Metre" adequate for poetic expression, yet Cowper managed to create a masterpiece within these limitations.

The heading for this hymn when it was first published was "Conflict. Light shining out of darkness", and it may well have been written in one of Cowper's blacker moments. While many hymns seek to explain faith, this one starts from the opposite viewpoint: that acts of God are beyond our comprehension. Not only are his "wonders" beyond our grasp, but the means of achieving them defy understanding. "O the depth of the riches both of the wisdom and knowledge of God! How unsearchable are his judgments, and his ways past finding out! For who hath known the mind of the Lord? or who hath been his counsellor?" (*Romans 11:33–34*).

This is the message of the Book of Job, which is one of the sources of inspiration for this hymn. There are also many allusions to the Psalms and to other biblical passages, but the unusual reference to mines in the second verse points to Job 28. In this chapter (best understood in a modern translation) there is an intriguing description of men mining for precious stones (*Job 28:1–11*), yet for all their ingenuity men cannot find wisdom (*vv.12–22*). Only God the Creator can reveal it (*vv.23–28*). The message of the epic poem which forms the Book of Job is that "God moves in a mysterious way . . ." (v.1.1): ". . . unto God would I commit my cause: Which doeth great things and unsearchable. . . ." (*Job 5:8–9*). ("Mysterious" has slightly changed its meaning: it used to mean "unsearchable" in Cowper's day.) Throughout the book, Job's friends and God himself point to creation to prove God's greatness (v.1.3–4). Cowper's first verse also refers to Psalm 104, and it reminds us of the time when Jesus walked on the Sea of Galilee after a storm, to the consternation of "fearful saints".

"Can you find out the deep things of God?" asks Zophar of Job (*Job 11:7*, RSV), a question repeated in different ways in many other parts of the same book. This could be a depressing thought—is God therefore unknowable? But God himself communicated with Job (v.6.3–4), pointing to his creation. This is Job's comfort—that he can communicate with God and is safe in the hands of the God who is all-powerful, all-knowing. So Cowper's thought moves from God's greatness (vv.1–2) to his providence (vv.3–6).

Verse 3 is an encouragement to all "fearful saints" who fear what *might* happen: threats may turn out to be blessings. God's mercy can be seen in the clouds that threaten devastation (v.3.2) yet bring the blessing of rain. In the arid land of Israel storms are indeed feared, yet every drop of water is precious. Verses 3 and 5 can be seen as a poet's rendering of God's words in the Book of Job: "Who hath divided . . . a way for the lightning of thunder; to cause it to rain on the earth . . . to cause the bud of the tender herb to spring forth?" (*Job 38:25–27*).

In verse 4, Cowper reminds us that our own "feeble sense" (v.4.1) is insufficient to understand our Creator, and calls us to "*trust* Him for His grace" (v.4.2). Faith, not reason, is at the centre of Christianity. Without belief we "scan His work in vain" (v.6.2). Thus we must trust God to interpret his work to us (v.6.3). "Do not interpretations belong to God?" (*Genesis 40:8*).

HAIL TO THE LORD'S ANOINTED
James Montgomery (1771–1854)

"Blessed be his glorious name for ever:
let the whole earth be filled with his glory"
(*Psalm 72:19*)

1 Hail to the Lord's Anointed!
  Great David's greater Son;
Hail, in the time appointed,
  His reign on earth begun!
He comes to break oppression,
  To set the captive free;
To take away transgression,
  And rule in equity.

2 He comes with succour speedy
  To those who suffer wrong;
To help the poor and needy,
  And bid the weak be strong;
To give them songs for sighing,
  Their darkness turn to light,
Whose souls, condemned and dying,
  Were precious in his sight.

3 He shall come down like showers
  Upon the fruitful earth,
And love, joy, hope, like flowers,
  Spring in his path to birth:
Before him on the mountains
  Shall peace the herald go;
And righteousness in fountains
  From hill to valley flow.

4 Arabia's desert-ranger
  To him shall bow the knee;
The Ethiopian stranger
  His glory come to see;
With offerings of devotion
  Ships from the isles shall meet,
To pour the wealth of ocean
  In tribute at his feet.

5 Kings shall fall down before him,
  And gold and incense bring;
All nations shall adore him,
  His praise all people sing;
To him shall prayer unceasing
  And daily vows ascend;
His kingdom still increasing,
  A kingdom without end.

6 O'er every foe victorious,
  He on His throne shall rest;
From age to age more glorious,
  All-blessing and all-blest.
The tide of time shall never
  His covenant remove;
His Name shall stand for ever;
  That name to us is Love.

James Montgomery (1771–1854) is one of the most remarkable men to feature in any hymn book. There is apparently no recent biography of this man, but his fascinating life is told briefly in Ch. 5 of "They wrote our hymns" by H. Martin (SCM Press, 1961). His father was a Moravian minister in Irvine, Ayrshire, and later a missionary in the West Indies, where he died when James was 12.

James worked in a baker's shop and a chandler's shop, then with the "Sheffield Register" newspaper. His talents led to him becoming its editor, a post he retained for 31 years. His radical writing on the French Revolution and on a political riot in Sheffield resulted in two periods of imprisonment. He wrote many poems, well received at the time, but now forgotten. Of his 400 hymns, several are still in use, for example: "Angels from the Realms of Glory"; "Songs of Praise the Angels sang"; "Stand up and bless the Lord"; "For ever with the Lord". "Hail to the Lord's Anointed" was written for a Christmas Ode, sung at a Moravian settlement in England in 1821. It was in print in 1822, but not in a hymn book until 1853, when Montgomery's "Original Hymns" was published.

Although based on Psalm 72, the hymn incorporates many New Testament concepts interwoven with words from the Psalms. Originally, there were eight verses; six is normally the maximum number sung at present.

Psalm 72 has long been recognised for its many references to the Messiah. The message of the first two verses of the hymn—of Jesus breaking oppression and freeing captives—echoes both the Psalm (72:2 & 4) and the passage from Isaiah that Jesus read and applied to himself in the synagogue (Luke 4:18): "He hath anointed me to preach the Gospel to the poor; he hath sent me to heal the broken-hearted, to preach deliverance to the captives, and recovering of sight to the blind, to set at liberty them that are bruised." The message of peace based on justice is found throughout Psalm 72. Montgomery has taken verse 4 of the psalm and linked it to verses 12–14 to create the second verse of his hymn.

Verse 3 of the hymn paints a beautiful picture of a peaceful world: "He shall come down like . . . showers that water the earth" (Psalm 72:6). The image at the end of the verse is partly from the prophet Amos (5:24): "Let judgment run down as waters, and righteousness as a mighty stream." But the detailed imagery is Montgomery's own. He wrote, "From hill to vale, the fountains of righteousness o'erflow." Most books now use the version first printed in Hymns Ancient and Modern, 1861: "And Righteousness like fountains, from hill to valley flow". Both forms are, in effect, a description of the rivers and waterfalls of the Pennines that were so close to his Sheffield home. The local scene provided a picture that is true to the spirit of the Psalm.

Verses 1 to 3 deal with the message of the Messiah. The wider context of the coming of the Messiah is the theme of verses 4 and 5. As the Righteous King, people from distant places recognise his authority. "They that dwell in the wilderness shall bow before him" says Psalm 72:9. In the hymn this becomes, appropriately, "Arabia's desert-ranger" (v.4.1). The presents of Kings (Psalm 72:10) are identified as the wise men's gifts of gold and incense (v.5.2). "Daily shall he be praised" (Psalm 72:15) becomes the "unceasing" prayers and vows of verse 5: a knowledge of the earth's rotation led Montgomery to recognise the never-ending nature of prayer and praise.

The final verse is firmly rooted in Psalm 72, in the Prophets, and in the New Testament. This covenant will never be removed (see Jeremiah 31:31–34). The last lines originally read: "His name shall stand for ever; His name—what is it?—Love." Montgomery himself changed it later to "That name to us is love". Some hymn books have further altered it to "His changeless name of love". "His name shall endure for ever" is in verse 17 of the Psalm; the title of Love comes from the New Testament. Thus the words (v.6.8) "to us" link closely with the idea of the "new covenant" which we can enjoy.

HOW SWEET THE NAME OF JESUS SOUNDS
John Newton (1725–1807)

"Thy name is as ointment poured forth"
(Song of Songs 1:3)

1 How sweet the name of Jesus sounds
  In a believer's ear!
 It soothes his sorrows, heals his
    wounds,
 And drives away his fear.

2 It makes the wounded spirit whole,
  And calms the troubled breast;
 'Tis manna to the hungry soul,
  And to the weary rest.

3 Dear name! the rock on which I build,
  My shield and hiding-place,
 My never-failing treasury filled
  With boundless stores of grace.

4 Jesus! my Shepherd, Husband, Friend,
  My Prophet, Priest, and King,
 My lord, my Life, my Way, my End,
  Accept the praise I bring.

5 Weak is the effort of my heart,
  And cold my warmest thought;
 But when I see thee as thou art,
  I'll praise thee as I ought.

6 Till then I would thy love proclaim
  With every fleeting breath;
 And may the music of thy name
  Refresh my soul in death.

John Newton's biography is better known than that of almost any other hymn-writer, probably because his was such a colourful life. He was born in 1725; his mother died when he was only 7; his father was a shipmaster, and at first John worked for him. Later, he was a midshipman on a man-o'-war, and was flogged for attempting to desert. He then worked on slave ships—the most degrading and inhuman trade ever undertaken by British vessels. He became master of a slave-ship even after his conversion to Christ, but later in his life he argued for the abolition of slavery. By 1764, he had become an Anglican curate at Olney, Bucks., and worked with Cowper on the "Olney Hymns" published in 1779. He died in 1807; the year that the slave trade was abolished in the British Empire.

24

This hymn was first published in "Olney Hymns" with the title "The Name of Jesus", and with the same verse of Scripture as given here. It is interesting to find an Old Testament verse used for a New Testament theme.

The first two verses speak of the many facets of faith in Jesus: sorrow is soothed . . . wounds are healed . . . fear is driven away . . . troubles are calmed . . . hunger is satisfied . . . weariness finds rest. Each of these ideas can be traced to verses in the Bible: some to Jesus' miracles of healing, others to the examples of changed lives in the Acts of the Apostles.

Verse 3 is helpful in combining the ideas of Jesus as both the rock on which to build, and also as a hiding-place. Logically, these are opposites, but both are biblical images and valid descriptions of faith. As the psalmist recognised, "God is our refuge and strength" (*Psalm 46:1*).

The first line of verse 4 was originally "Shepherd, Husband, Friend". The idea of Husband may come from the Song of Songs, along with the text for the hymn. "Husband" is also found in the New Testament, but always in the context of the Church (not the individual) as the Bride of Christ. Thus "Husband" has been changed in many hymn books. The variety of alternatives chosen is an apt illustration of the many ways Christians can speak of Christ: Leader; Surety; Brother; Guardian; Saviour—all these have been printed in hymn books. This verse offers contrasts as marked as verse 3, and again these apparent paradoxes embody essential Christian concepts: "My Shepherd" is "My King" as well; "my Prophet" is also "my Friend"; "my Way" is also "my End". Each word can be found in the Bible, and each word merits reflection.

After this magnificent collection of titles of Christ it is encouraging to find that even a man such as Newton can write such a profound and personal verse, acknowledging that his thought is cold and his efforts weak. Relatively few hymns recognise our lack of responsiveness, and verse 5 must be treasured by many people. Nevertheless, the author is resolved to praise Jesus continually (verse 6). One Brethren hymn book has amended the conclusion to give the hymn a more positive close:

"And triumph in thy blessed name,
Which quells the power of death."

I WILL GO IN THE STRENGTH OF THE LORD
Edward Turney (1816–1872)

"I will go in the strength of the Lord"
(Psalm 71:16)

1 I will go in the strength of the Lord
   In the path He hath mark'd for my feet:
I will follow the light of His word,
   Nor shrink from the dangers I meet.
His presence my steps shall attend;
   His fulness my wants shall supply;
On Him, till my journey shall end,
   My hope shall securely rely.

2 I will go in the strength of the Lord
   To the work He appoints me to do;
In the joy which His smile shall afford
   My soul shall her vigour renew.
His wisdom will guard me from harm,
   His pow'r my sufficiency prove;
I will trust His omnipotent arm,
   I will rest in His covenant love.

Edward Turney was an American Baptist minister. He was born in Easton, Connecticut in 1816 and graduated from Madison University, New York. He was pastor in Hartford and Granville, Ohio, and in 1850 he became Professor of Biblical Criticism in Madison University. He held other teaching posts, and died in Washington in 1872. During his life he published two books of hymns. "I will go in the strength of the Lord" was written about 1860 and originally had three verses.

This hymn takes a phrase from the Psalms, and uses those exact words as the first line of each verse, and as the key theme for the whole hymn. The rhythm of the phrase is "Anapaestic" ($\times \times -$), hence each verse follows this unusual rhythm. Besides this repeated phrase of Scripture, almost every line of the hymn can be traced to a biblical verse, often from the Psalms.

The author believes that God has a path for him (v.1.2): "He leadeth me in the paths of righteousness" (*Psalm 23:3*). His word gives the light for us to see the way (v.1.3): "Thy word is a light unto my path" (*Psalm 119:105*). Confidence in His presence (v.1.5) means that dangers do not frighten: 'I will fear no evil, for thou art with me" (*Psalm 23:4*). "His fullness my wants shall supply" (v.1.6) is perhaps based on "God shall supply all your need according to his riches" (*Philippians 4.19*).

Verse 2 starts from the same point, but recognises that there is work to be done (v.2.2). We can trust God's omnipotent wisdom and power (v.2.5–7) to be sufficient for us: "My grace is sufficient for thee, for my strength is made perfect in weakness" (*2 Corinthians 12:9*). It is noteworthy that work (v.2.2) and rest (v.2.8) can be spoken of in the same verse—a great contrast to the general attitude that work and leisure are poles apart. There is inner "rest" in the confidence of God's presence, and the Christian can see all his life—work and leisure—as one. These two verses are a remarkably clear and positive expression of the Christian life, so it is puzzling that so few hymn books include this hymn.

IMMORTAL LOVE, FOREVER FULL
John Greenleaf Whittier (1807–1892)

"One is your Master, even Christ"
(*Matthew 23:8*)

1 Immortal Love, forever full,
    Forever flowing free,
Forever shared, forever whole,
    A never-ebbing sea!

2 Our outward lips confess the Name
    All other names above;
Love only knoweth whence it came,
    And comprehendeth love.

3 We may not climb the heavenly steeps
    To bring the Lord Christ down;
In vain we search the lowest deeps,
    For Him no depths can drown.

4 But warm, sweet, tender, even yet
    A present help is He;
And faith has still its Olivet,
    And love its Galilee.

5 The healing of His seamless dress
    Is by our beds of pain;
We touch Him in life's throng and press,
    And we are whole again.

6 Through Him the first fond prayers are
    said
    Our lips of childhood frame,
The last low whispers of our dead
    Are burdened with His Name.

7 O Lord and Master of us all!
    Whate'er our name or sign,
We own Thy sway, we hear Thy
    call,
    We test our lives by Thine.

8 We faintly hear, we dimly see,
    In differing phrase we pray;
But, dim or clear, we learn of Thee
    The Light, the Truth, the Way.

9 Alone, O Love ineffable,
    Thy saving Name is given;
To turn aside from Thee is hell,
    To walk with Thee is heaven!

John Greenleaf Whittier was a farmer's son, living in New England, U.S.A. At first he worked on his father's farm—hence, perhaps, his feeling for beauty and peace. Later he became a poet and a newspaper editor, writing not only poems but also anti-slavery propaganda. Whittier was a member of the Society of Friends, or Quakers. He did not write hymns: the poems have subsequently been adapted for use as hymns. Among his other well-known poems which have become hymns are "O brother man, fold to thy heart thy brother", and "Dear Lord and Father of Mankind"—an extract from a long poem entitled "The Brewing of Soma". In that poem, he compared superficial, emotional Christianity with the taking of an Indian drug.

As with all hymns by John Greenleaf Whittier, this was written as a poem, not a hymn. Its title was "OUR MASTER", and the text above it here is the same as in the original edition of the poem. There were originally 35 verses and different hymn books have selected different parts of the poem—ranging from six verses in "Christian Praise" to fifteen in "Congregational Praise"! But whichever parts are printed, the hymn emphasises from beginning to end man's lack of ability to comprehend Jesus Christ. How *can* his love be "forever shared" *and* "forever whole"? Nor can we find him through objective exploration— but only through experience (vv.3–4).

Whittier's recognition of the *incomprehensible* dimension of faith is remarkably modern—even though he wrote the hymn while rigid belief was still largely unchallenged. His vision of hell was not of literal hell-fire, nor was his heaven literal harp-playing (v.9). What better definition of a modern Christian faith is there than this?

He sees Christian faith as something intangible, with many differences—and differences in style of worship from person to person are not necessarily right or wrong (v.8.2). He recognises that our hearing and sight are only partial (v.8.1), but all Christians are united in our allegiance to Christ (v.7.3–4), who is "Love ineffable" (v.9.1).

JESUS CALLS US; O'ER THE TUMULT
Cecil Frances Alexander (1823–95)

"He saith unto them, Follow Me."
(Matthew 4.19)

1 Jesus calls us; o'er the tumult
    Of our life's wild restless sea
Day by day His sweet voice soundeth,
    Saying, "Christian, follow Me."

2 As of old, St. Andrew heard it
    By the Galilean lake,
Turned from home and toil and kindred,
    Leaving all for His dear sake.

3 Jesus calls us from the worship
    Of the vain world's golden store,
From each idol that would keep us,
    Saying, "Christian, love Me more."

4 In our joys and in our sorrows,
    Days of toil and hours of ease,
Still He calls, in cares and pleasures,
    "Christian, love Me more than these."

5 Jesus calls us: by Thy mercies,
    Saviour, may we hear Thy call,
Give our hearts to Thine obedience,
    Serve and love Thee best of all.

Mrs. C. F. Alexander (1823–1895) was the wife of a Church of Ireland clergyman, who served in a remote Donegal parish, then as Bishop of Derry, and finally as Archbishop of Armagh and Primate of All Ireland. She published several hymns for children, to interpret for them the basic truths of Christianity. Among her other well-known hymns are "All things bright and beautiful", "Once in Royal David's city" and "There is a green hill far away".

The concept of the "call" is central to this hymn: the word appears in every verse except one. It is an idea that is much older than Christ's earthly ministry when he called disciples.

In the Old Testament "the call" usually refers to the call of prophets. Jesus called individuals during his life on earth—individuals such as St. Andrew the fisherman. Verse 2 often refers to "the apostles", but originally Mrs. Alexander wrote the hymn for St. Andrew's day, November 30th. She took the idea of the call to speak not just of St. Andrew, but to speak to everyone who sings the hymn. This is one of the few Saint's Day hymns which merits use throughout the year.

The "wild, restless sea" (v.1.2) refers both literally to Andrew's work as a fisherman on the Sea of Galilee where storms can suddenly break out, and also metaphorically to our lives. The simple, calm message, "Follow me", contrasts markedly with that restlessness.

The call is *to* Christ (v.1), but in St. Andrew's case this was a call *from* home and kindred (v.2.3)—in fact, from everything in his previous life (v.2.4). Similarly it is a call *from* our gold and idols. The author leaves each reader to work out what he or she may be making into an idol by putting it in God's rightful place. This call is more important than both our work and our leisure (v.4.2)—we may not be called to leave them, but we are certainly called to get our priorities right (v.4.4). And we can ask Jesus, the Caller, to help us (v.5.1−2): we are not alone in the struggle.

31

JESU, THOU JOY OF LOVING HEARTS

"He satisfieth the longing soul"
(Psalm 107:9)

1 Jesu, Thou Joy of loving hearts,
   Thou Fount of life, Thou Light of men;
From the best bliss that earth imparts
   We turn unfilled to Thee again.

2 Thy truth unchanged hath ever stood;
   Thou savest those that on Thee call;
To them that seek Thee Thou art good,
   To them that find Thee, All in all.

3 We taste Thee, O Thou living Bread,
   And long to feast upon Thee still;
We drink of Thee, the Fountain Head,
   And thirst our souls from Thee to fill.

4 Our restless spirits yearn for Thee
   Where'er our changeful lot is cast;
Glad when Thy gracious smile we see,
   Blest when our faith can hold Thee fast.

5 O Jesus, ever with us stay;
   Make all our moments calm and bright;
Chase the dark night of sin away;
   Shed o'er the world Thy holy light.

In the past, this Latin hymn was attributed to St. Bernard of Clairvaux, but the words have since been found in a manuscript of the 11th century—too early for St. Bernard. It was used in liturgies in England and France in the 16th century, and in some versions it has 50 verses: we sing only a few today.

This translation from the Latin is by Ray Palmer (1808–1887), an American Congregational minister. Another translation of the same hymn appears as "Jesu, the very thought of thee", translated by E. Caswall in 1858; in some hymn books this has 15 verses. There is also J. M. Neale's version, "Jesus the very thought is sweet".

This hymn starts with Jesus as joy, life and light—by contrast with "the best bliss of earth" which leaves our longings unfilled. Although written 900 years ago, the concept is exceptionally meaningful today: the modern phrase "the bright lights" means precisely "the best bliss that life imparts". Verse 2 speaks of "unchanged truth"—another contrast with "earth's bliss", which changes so radically from year to year. One of the promises of that "unchanged" truth is set out in the rest of verse 2, reminding us of the promise of Jesus, "Ask, and it shall be given you; seek, and ye shall find; knock and it shall be opened unto you. . . ." (*Matthew 7:7–8*).

The next verse in that chapter of Matthew (*Matthew 7:9*) tells of a man asking for bread, and verse 3 of the hymn speaks of the "living bread". It is this verse which is the main reason that the hymn is often sung at communion services. Yet Jesus' statement, "I am the bread of life", was made long before the Last Supper (*John 6:35*). Jesus spoke of satisfaction, yet this hymn speaks of continued longing. It seems probable that the real source of the author's thoughts is a verse from the Apocrypha which is relatively unknown to people today: "They that eat me [Wisdom] shall yet be hungry, and they that drink me shall yet be thirsty" (*Ecclesiasticus 24:21*). This use of Old Testament imagery for a New Testament truth is a characteristic of many early hymns.

Verse 4 speaks of our restless yearnings. Here too the 11th-century author seems to be speaking with a 20th-century voice: the quest for fulfilment and for meaning in life is a constant theme today. And "our changeful lot" is truly prophetic: moving job and moving home is far more common now than it was then.

The end of verse 4 is most encouraging, and a good antidote to the over-certain and extravagant claims about faith of some more recent hymns. The author was glad when he was "in contact" with God, but accepted that sometimes he would feel distance and estrangement. Thus the author concludes his hymn with a prayer (v.5.1) for Jesus' presence with us, and for his calmness (v.5.2)—a good antidote to 20th-century stress. But this prayer does not stay at the personal level: it moves to request God's presence throughout his world. It recognises that our faith is both personal, inward experience, and also relevant to the world as a whole.

Let us, with a gladsome mind
John Milton (1608–1674)

"O give thanks unto the Lord; for he is good:
for his mercy endureth for ever."
(Psalm 136:1)

1 Let us, with a gladsome mind,
 Praise the Lord, for he is kind:
  For his mercies ay endure,
  Ever faithful, ever sure.

2 Let us blaze his name abroad,
 For of gods he is the God:

3 He with all-commanding might
 Filled the new-made world with light:

4 He the golden-tressed sun
 Caused all day his course to run:

5 The hornèd moon to shine by night,
 'Mid her spangled sisters bright:

6 He his chosen race did bless
 In the wasteful wilderness:

7 He hath, with a piteous eye,
 Looked upon our misery:

8 All things living he doth feed,
 His full hand supplies their need:

9 Let us then with gladsome mind,
 Praise the Lord, for he is kind:

This hymn was written by John Milton when he was only 15 years old, and still at St. Paul's School in London. The simple and direct style of the poem has made it a popular hymn.

John Milton was born in 1608, and survived both Cromwell's Commonwealth and the Restoration, despite his numerous political writings. From 1652 until his death in 1674 he was totally blind, and yet it was in these years that he wrote "Paradise Lost" and "Paradise Regained". He rendered nineteen psalms into verse, but only two others are in current use as hymns: "How lovely are thy dwellings fair" (*Psalm 84*) and "The Lord will come, and not be slow" (*Psalms 85 and 86*). None was originally intended as a hymn.

It is a strange irony that this hymn—Milton's simplest poem—is probably his best-known work. Millions of people remember it with pleasure from school or Sunday School, while his great poems appeal only to a minority.

34

This hymn is closely based on *Psalm 136*. The psalm has 26 verses, and Milton's poem originally had 22 verses. Hence, it is only a small proportion of Milton's poem that is sung today; the selection of verses varies considerably from one hymn book to another.

The psalm is clearly designed with responses: every verse concludes with the moving words, "For His mercy endureth for ever". Milton has adopted the same style in his hymn. The psalm starts with praise to God, for his goodness and greatness: ". . . the God of gods; . . . the Lord of lords" (*vv.2–3*), or in Milton's words "For of gods he is the God" (v.2.2).

God the Creator is praised in verses 4 to 9 of the psalm: "To him that by wisdom made the heavens . . . To him that stretched out the earth above the waters . . .". Milton draws this together in verse 3, perhaps the finest verse in the hymn. God is then praised as the saviour of Israel, in verses 10 to 24 of *Psalm 136*. Milton did not omit the details of Israel's history, but the only verse now used is verse 6. Many verses are long forgotten, and perhaps best forgotten, too, such as:

"In bloody battail he brought down
Kings of prowess and renown"

"And large-lim'd OG he did subdue
With all his over-hardy crew."

Finally, the Psalmist praises God, "Who giveth food to all flesh". Thus the vision widens to embrace the whole world, and verse 8 of the hymn makes it appropriate for harvest services as well as for all services of thanksgiving.

NATURE WITH OPEN VOLUME STANDS
Isaac Watts (1674–1748)

"The invisible things of Him from the creation of the world are clearly seen, being understood by the things that are made"
(Romans 1:20)

1 Nature with open volume stands,
    To spread her Maker's praise abroad;
And every labour of His hands
    Shows something worthy of a God.

2 But in the grace that rescued man,
    His brightest form of glory shines;
Here, on the cross, 'tis fairest drawn
    In precious blood and crimson lines.

3 Here His whole name appears complete:
    Nor wit can guess, nor reason prove
Which of the letters best is writ,
    The power, the wisdom, or the love.

4 Here I behold His inmost heart,
    Where grace and vengeance strangely join,
Piercing His Son with sharpest smart,
    To make the purchased pleasures mine.

5 Oh the sweet wonders of that cross
    Where Christ my Saviour loved and died!
Her noblest life my spirit draws
    From His dear wounds, and piercèd side.

6 I would for ever speak His name
    In sounds to mortal ears unknown;
With angels join to praise the Lamb,
    And worship at His Father's throne.

Isaac Watts deserves a whole book to himself: he wrote about 600 hymns, and well over 30 of these are outstanding enough still to be in regular use. He is not only one of the greatest hymn-writers; he was also the author of a standard university text on Logic, which was used for over a century.

His father was a nonconformist—an Independent—who attended Above Bar Congregational Church in Southampton; a church which is still very active. Isaac was born in 1674, when his father was still in prison for his beliefs. He refused university education because of the requirement of conformity to the Church of England, and studied instead at the Nonconformist Academy in London. After some years as a private tutor, he became an assistant at Mark Lane Independent Chapel, London, and in 1702 became Minister there. His first book of hymns was published in 1707, and contained "Nature with open volume stands". In 1712 he became seriously ill, and for 36 years until his death in 1748 he was a semi-invalid, living at Sir Thomas Abney's home at Theobalds, near Cheshunt, Herts., where he was tutor to the children.

This hymn starts with the praise of God as Creator. Verse 1 is reminiscent of many of the Psalms, which were the main form of praise in Watts's youth. Every aspect of nature reflects God; this verse speaks to everyone—even urbanised man, who can still see the sky and who so often longs for the country. Verse 1 is not sufficient in itself as a hymn of Christian praise, therefore verse 2 starts significantly with the word "But".

Watts was, in his time, a revolutionary influence on worship. The Psalms only spoke of a coming Messiah: they could not praise Jesus Christ as God. Watts speaks directly of "the grace that rescued man" (v.2.1), a key concept in Paul's epistles. The message of the cross is summed up (v.3.4) as power, wisdom and love—a reflection of Paul's phrase, "Christ, the power of God, and the wisdom of God" (*1 Corinthians 1:24*). The hymn was originally entitled "Wonders of the Cross".

Verse 4 has been deleted from some hymn books, but the image of vengeance speaks not of an arbitrary and unpredictable God, but of righteous condemnation of sin. "Vengeance is mine . . . saith the Lord" comes in the New Testament (*Romans 12:19*). And we need to reflect on God's judgment if we are to understand his grace in Christ. Line 4 of this verse probably refers to *Romans 8:32*: "He that spared not his own son . . . how shall he not with him also freely give us all things?"

We cannot fully grasp the meaning of the Crucifixion: Watts aptly reminds us of this in the phrases "grace and vengeance strangely join" (v.4.2), and "the sweet wonders of the Cross" (v.5.1). But we can recognise that his spirit—and ours—draws "noblest life" from the cross (v.5.3–4). So the hymn moves forward (v.6) to think of praising and worshipping God for ever.

O PRAISE YE THE LORD
Henry Baker (1821–1877)

"Praise ye the Lord . . . Praise ye him, all his angels"
(Psalm 148:1, 2)

1 O praise ye the Lord!
   Praise him in the height;
Rejoice in his word,
   Ye angels of light;
Ye heavens, adore him
   By whom ye were made,
And worship before him,
   In brightness arrayed.

2 O praise ye the Lord!
   Praise him upon earth,
In tuneful accord,
   Ye sons of new birth;
Praise him who hath brought you
   His grace from above,
Praise him who hath taught you
   To sing of his love.

3 O praise ye the Lord,
   All things that give sound;
Each jubilant chord,
   Re-echo around;
Loud organs, his glory
   Forth tell in deep tone,
And sweet harp, the story
   Of what he hath done.

4 O praise ye the Lord!
   Thanksgiving and song
To him be outpoured
   All ages along:
For love in creation,
   For heaven restored,
For grace of salvation,
   Oh praise ye the Lord!

Sir Henry Baker (1821–1877) was the son of a Vice-Admiral. He went to Cambridge University, and was vicar of Monkland, Herefordshire, for his whole life. He was the Chairman of the Editorial Committee of "Hymns Ancient and Modern". Other well-known hymns of his are "The King of Love my Shepherd is" and "Lord, thy word abideth". As well as writing hymns, he also translated a number from Latin and German.

Victorian hymns are often thought nowadays to be sentimental, even "slushy". Some undoubtedly are—but the generalisation is most misleading. There is nothing sentimental about this simple, yet profound, hymn of praise. Although all reference books state that this hymn is a paraphrase of the final psalm (*Psalm 150*), verse 1 is in fact closely based on *Psalm 148:1-2*:

"Praise ye the Lord. Praise ye the Lord from the heavens: praise him in the heights. Praise ye him, all his angels."

At first sight, verse 1 may seem irrelevant: angels seem so distant from a materialistic age. But the author's lines "Rejoice in His Word . . . adore Him by whom ye were made, and worship before Him . . ." apply equally to us on earth. Thus this becomes a prelude to verse 2, which speaks directly to us, and expresses God's twin gifts of salvation and of intelligence to respond to him.

In verse 3, the theme comes from *Psalm 150*: music is a means of praising God. The final verse invites praise for creation and restoration and salvation: thus an apparently simple hymn holds the essence of the Christian message.

PRAISE, MY SOUL, THE KING OF HEAVEN
Henry Francis Lyte (1793–1847)

"My soul shall praise the King of Heaven"
(*Tobit 13:7*)

1 Praise, my soul, the King of heaven;
  To his feet thy tribute bring.
Ransomed, healed, restored, forgiven,
  Who like me his praise should sing?
  Praise him! Praise him!
Praise the everlasting King.

2 Praise him for his grace and favour
  To our fathers in distress;
Praise him still the same for ever,
  Slow to chide, and swift to bless.
  Praise him! Praise him!
Glorious in his faithfulness.

3 Father-like, he tends and spares us;
  Well our feeble frame he knows;
In his hands he gently bears us,
  Rescues us from all our foes.
  Praise him! Praise him!
Widely as his mercy flows.

4 Frail as summer's flower we flourish;
  Blows the wind and it is gone;
But while mortals rise and flourish,
  God endures unchanging on.
  Praise him! Praise him!
Praise the high eternal one.

5 Angels, help us to adore him;
  Ye behold him face to face;
Sun and moon, bow down before him;
  Dwellers all in time and space.
  Praise him! Praise him!
Praise with us the God of grace

Henry Francis Lyte published this hymn in 1834 in his now almost forgotten book, "Spirit of the Psalms". Few of the other hymns from this book are now in common use, even though it included over 280 items. The other well-known one is "God of Mercy, God of Grace", based on Psalm 67, and a few hymn books include "Praise the Lord, His glories show" (*Psalm 150*) and "Whom should we love but Thee" (*Psalm 18*). The author is best-known for another hymn which is not based on a Psalm: "Abide with me".

Lyte was born in 1793 at Ednam, near Kelso, in the Southern Uplands of Scotland, the son of an army captain. He was educated in Ireland, at the Royal School of Enniskillen, County Fermanagh; and then at Trinity College, Dublin, an Anglican establishment. He was clearly a most talented person: he originally planned to be a doctor, yet won three prizes for poetry. Ordained in 1815, he served his first curacy at Taghmon, near Wexford in south-east Ireland. After 2 years he moved to Marazion, Cornwall, and from 1823 he was curate at the fishing village of Lower Brixham in South Devon. He died on November 20th, 1847, in Nice, where he had gone because of failing health. Exactly a hundred years later, on November 20th, 1947, Queen Elizabeth II (when still Princess Elizabeth) and Prince Philip chose this hymn for the opening processional at their wedding.

40

B ased mainly on Psalm 103, this is not a paraphrase, but a re-expression of the Psalmist's thinking, seen in the light of the New Testament. There are several other quotations from Scripture that are little known today. The term "King of Heaven", and a number of other phrases, are from the Book of Tobit in the Apocrypha: Then Tobit wrote a prayer of rejoicing, and said (*Tobit 13:1*) . . . "My soul shall praise the *King of Heaven*" (*Tobit 13.7*) . . . "Give praise to the Lord . . . and *praise the everlasting King*" (*Tobit 13:10*). (See v.1.6.) "To his feet thy tribute bring" (v.1.2) is another phrase from the same chapter of Tobit (*13:11*): "Many nations shall come from far to the name of the Lord God, with gifts in their hands; even gifts to the King of Heaven". This whole chapter of Tobit is an outstanding prayer of praise.

The four verbs of line 3 of the first verse make an unforgettable impact on all who think about the hymn as they sing it. *Psalm 103:3–4* use the words "forgiveth . . . healeth . . . redeemeth". In the context of Christianity, this one line is a remarkable summary of our faith.

The Psalmist praises God for his "acts to the children of Israel" (*Psalm 103:7*); the hymn-writer widens this idea to "our fathers" (v.2.2). Grace and mercy (favour) are present in both psalm and hymn, and both the psalmist (*103:8*) and the hymn-writer (v.2.4) praise the Lord because he is slow to anger. The phrase, "still the same for ever", refers to *Psalm 103:17*, "the mercy of the Lord is from everlasting to everlasting", but there is also a hint of the New Testament verse, "Jesus Christ, the same yesterday and today and forever" (*Hebrews 13:8*).

Verse 3 moves to the concept of God as father: a remarkable metaphor that is closely based on this Psalm. This is one of many places in the Old Testament where this analogy is used, yet the idea remains widespread that the God of the Old Testament was remote. "Like as a father pitieth his children, so the Lord pitieth them that fear him. For he knoweth our frame; he remembereth that we are but dust" (*Psalm 103:13–14*).

Lyte's original verse 4 is often omitted from hymn books, even though it is closely based on *Psalm 103:15–17*. The contrast of the first and second couplets is particularly noteworthy.

The final verse moves to God as the great Creator. The ideas of God the Creator and God the Father can seem almost contradictory to non-Christians, but this hymn blends the two concepts by making a free rendering of *Psalm 103:20–21*: "Bless the Lord, ye his angels . . . Bless the Lord, all ye his hosts". Angels, and the sun and moon, are invited to join with us in praising the God of grace. (See also *Psalm 148:2–3*.) Some hymn books render lines 3 and 4 as "Saints triumphant bow before him, Gathered in from every race": this version, too, effectively conveys the idea of heaven and earth together praising the Lord.

PRAISE TO THE HOLIEST IN THE HEIGHT
John Henry Newman (1801–1890)

". . . the second Man is the Lord from Heaven"
(1 Corinthians 15:47)

---

1 Praise to the Holiest in the height,
  And in the depth be praise,
 In all his words most wonderful,
  Most sure in all his ways.

2 O loving wisdom of our God!
  When all was sin and shame,
 A second Adam to the fight
  And to the rescue came.

3 O wisest love! that flesh and blood
  Which did in Adam fail,
 Should strive afresh against the foe,
  Should strive and should prevail.

4 And that a higher gift than grace
  Should flesh and blood refine,
 God's presence and his very Self,
  And Essence all-divine.

5 O generous love! that he who smote
  In Man for man the foe,
 The double agony in Man
  For man should undergo;

6 And in the garden secretly,
  And on the Cross on high,
 Should teach his brethren, and inspire
  To suffer and to die.

7 Praise to the Holiest in the height,
  And in the depth be praise,
 In all his words most wonderful,
  Most sure in all his ways.

John Henry Newman (1801–1890) was the son of a London banker. He became a student and don at Oxford, vicar of the University Church, and was a leading Anglo-Catholic. In 1845 he left the Church of England and became a Roman Catholic, eventually becoming a Cardinal. His other well-known hymn is "Lead kindly light", and he also wrote many poems.

This hymn is taken from a long and complex work, "The Dream of Gerontius", where it is sung by the choir of angels as the soul of Gerontius is taken to judgment. Much of the theology in "The Dream" is very complex and acceptable only to Roman Catholics, yet this hymn is found in almost all hymn books—Roman Catholic, Anglican and Free Church. Its wide appeal comes partly from the simple majesty of the first verse, repeated at the end. This verse unites all Christendom in praising God for His words and ways. The hymn then goes on to expound God's ways.

Verses 2 to 6 are probably the most complex expressions of Christian truth in any hymn book. Although the words are simple, and the verses are short, the meaning is profound, and not always easy to follow.

Verses 2 and 3 refer to Christ, "the second Adam" (v.2.3 and *1 Corinthians 15:45*) coming to rescue us from sin and shame (v.2.2). Flesh and blood in the first Adam failed to obey God (v.3.1–2). But Christ's personal coming in "flesh and blood", prevails over sin (v.3.3–4).

Having sung of the humanity of Christ, verse 4 moves to his divinity. Jesus is truly God: "His Essence all divine" (v.4.4)—the capital letters are vital. Thus there is the double agony (v.5.3) of the Crucifixion: the physical agony of Jesus as Man, and the spiritual agony of bearing sin, undergone "in Man for man", that is, for the sake of mankind. "Man" with a capital "M" cannot be sung differently from "man", but this is the key to understanding verse 5.

Christ thus becomes our example: he teaches both when with his disciples secretly, in the Garden of Gethsemane (v.6.1), and publicly on the cross (v.6.2). Through the centuries he has inspired people to follow him, through suffering and even through death. And so the final verse repeats verse 1, praising God for his wonderful words and deeds. Because of the context of "The Dream", from which the words are taken, the hymn does not mention the Resurrection directly—even though there are several references to *1 Corinthians 15* which has resurrection as its theme.

REJOICE, THE LORD IS KING!
Charles Wesley (1707–1788)

"Rejoice in the Lord alway; and again I say, Rejoice"
(Philippians 4:4)

---

1 Rejoice, the Lord is King!
    Your Lord and King adore,
Mortals, give thanks, and sing,
    And triumph evermore:
Lift up your heart, lift up your voice,
Rejoice, again I say, rejoice.

2 Jesus the Saviour reigns,
    The God of truth and love;
When he had purged our stains,
    He took his seat above:
Lift up your heart, lift up your voice,
Rejoice, again I say, rejoice.

3 His kingdom cannot fail,
    He rules o'er earth and heaven;
The keys of death and hell
    Are to our Jesus given:
Lift up your heart, lift up your voice,
Rejoice, again I say, rejoice.

4 He sits at God's right hand,
    Till all his foes submit,
And bow to his command,
    And fall beneath his feet:
Lift up your heart, lift up your voice,
Rejoice, again I say, rejoice.

5 He all his foes shall quell,
    Shall all our sins destroy,
And every bosom swell
    With pure seraphic joy;
Lift up your heart, lift up your voice,
Rejoice, again I say, rejoice.

6 Rejoice in glorious hope,
    Jesus the Judge shall come,
And take his servants up
    To their eternal home:
We soon shall hear the archangel's voice,
The trump of God shall sound, Rejoice!

Charles Wesley (1707–1788) wrote over 6000 hymns, and most hymn books have more hymns written by him than by any other author. The preface to the "Methodist Hymn Book" begins "Methodism was born in song". Charles worked with his brother John to preach and teach throughout Britain and Ireland, but while John was the traveller and organiser, Charles expressed their beliefs in verse.

"Rejoice, the Lord is King" is one of the best-known of Charles Wesley's hymns. It was originally published in 1744, in his "Moral and Sacred Poems" and two years later appeared in a pamphlet entitled "Hymns for our Lord's Resurrection". It was always regarded as an Easter hymn, so was not included in John Wesley's "Hymns for the use of the people called Methodists" of 1780, as there were no special sections for the Christian Year. That hymn book went through many editions, but this hymn was not added until the 1875 Supplement. All 6 verses are still in the Methodist Hymn Book, although most other books now omit verse 5, and many also omit verse 6.

The tune "Gopsal" is almost inseparable from the words—and rightly so, for it was specially written to fit these words by none other than G. F. Handel.

Rejoice! is a fine start to a hymn for Easter Day—and for all other days. It is now recognised as a hymn of praise for all the year. In worship we adore (v.1.2), we give thanks (v.1.3), we sing (v.1.3), and we triumph (v.1.4). The refrain uses three verses of Scripture, from widely different sources, to express our praise to God: *Philippians 4* (quoted opposite), *Lamentations 3:41*, "Let us lift up our hearts . . . unto God in the Heavens", and *Isaiah 40:9*, "Lift up thy voice with strength: lift it up, be not afraid; say unto the cities of Judah, Behold your God." This hymn well illustrates Charles Wesley's marvellous ability to draw texts from many parts of Scripture to illustrate one theme.

We rejoice both because of Jesus' present reign (vv.2–3) and his future triumph (vv.4–6). Verse 2 speaks of the present-day kingship of Jesus. Wesley rephrases a verse from the beginning of the Epistle to the Hebrews: "When (Jesus) had by himself purged our sins, he sat down on the right hand of the Majesty on high" (*Hebrews 1:3*).

"A kingdom which cannot be removed" (*Hebrews 12:28*) becomes in the hymn, "His kingdom cannot fail" (v.3.1). The contrast with human kingdoms is even clearer today than when Wesley wrote, in the relative calm of the 18th century. "I have the keys of hell and of death" (v.3.3–4) is from *Revelation 1:18*. The well-known words of Paul in *Philippians 2:10* are re-expressed in verse 4: "God hath highly exalted him . . . at the name of Jesus, every knee shall bow, of things in heaven and things in earth and things under the earth, and every tongue confess that Jesus Christ is Lord".

The "foes" of verse 4.2 are explained further in verse 5.1–2. These are the foes of sin and evil which the Christian is exhorted to fight (*Ephesians 6:12*). Our rejoicing is not at the expense of other people, as in human wars, for *our* sins are included among the foes in verse 5.2!

So verse 6 looks forward to the "glorious hope"; as in so many of Wesley's hymns, the last verse concerns the second coming of Christ. It paraphrases *1 Thessalonians 4:16–17*, "The Lord himself shall descend from heaven with a shout, with the voice of the archangel, and with the trump of God . . . so shall we ever be with the Lord". Thus the hymn ends as it started—*Rejoice!*

SOULS OF MEN! WHY WILL YE SCATTER
F. W. Faber (1814–1863)

"I came not to judge the world, but to save the world"
(John 12:47)

---

1 Souls of men! why will ye scatter
    Like a crowd of frightened sheep?
Foolish hearts! why will ye wander
    From a love so true and deep?

2 Was there ever kindest shepherd
    Half so gentle, half so sweet
As the Saviour Who would have us
    Come and gather round His feet?

3 There's a wideness in God's mercy
    Like the wideness of the sea:
There's a kindness in His justice
    Which is more than liberty.

4 There is no place where earth's sorrows
    Are more felt than up in heaven;
There is no place where earth's failings
    Have such kindly judgment given.

5 For the love of God is broader
    Than the measures of man's mind;
And the heart of the Eternal
    Is most wonderfully kind.

6 But we make His love too narrow
    By false limits of our own;
And we magnify His strictness
    With a zeal He will not own.

7 There is plentiful redemption
    In the blood that has been shed;
There is joy for all the members
    In the sorrows of the Head.

8 If our love were but more simple
    We should take Him at His word;
And our lives would be all sunshine
    In the sweetness of our Lord.

F. W. Faber was born in 1814, and brought up as a Calvinist in Calverley, Yorkshire. He was educated at Shrewsbury and Harrow and at Oxford University, where he became a Fellow of University College in 1837. He was rector of Elton, Huntingdonshire (now Cambridgeshire) from 1842 to 1845, but then joined the Roman Catholic Church, first in Birmingham and then in London. He published several volumes of hymns, and his aim was to write hymns for Catholics with the same popular appeal as Cowper's and Newton's "Olney Hymns". His best hymns now appeal equally to non-Catholics. Faber died in 1863.

Thirteen verses are too many to sing. That is the limit of the agreement among hymn-book editors in regard to this hymn. Almost every book has a different selection of verses, and, alone among hymns, there are three different "first verses":

"Souls of men, why will ye scatter . . ." (Faber's original, as in "Hymns Ancient & Modern"; "Christian Praise"; Christian Worship"; etc.).

"Was there ever kindest shepherd . . ." (as in "Congregational Praise", etc.).

"There's a wideness in God's mercy . . ." (as in "Songs of Praise"; "English Hymnal"; etc.).

Thus, many hymn books omit one half, or the other half, or all of the description of mankind as scattered, frightened sheep, and Jesus as the kind and gentle shepherd.

In fact, this description is a most helpful analogy and is firmly rooted in the Bible. *Psalm 23:1* must be one of the best-known Scripture verses. Children can grasp the idea of the sheep and the shepherd, yet adults can find further depth. As well as *Isaiah 53* and *John 10*, there is the Bible verse which may be the origin of Faber's first verse: "When he saw the multitudes, he was moved with compassion on them, because they fainted, and were scattered abroad, as sheep having no shepherd" (*Matthew 9:36*).

The close relationship of shepherd and sheep is not alone sufficient, however, as a description of God. The "wideness in God's mercy" (v.3.1) needs another simile: the wideness of the sea. "If . . . I dwell in the uttermost parts of the sea; even there shall thy hand lead me, and thy right hand shall hold me" (*Psalm 139:9–10*).

Each verse brings out another aspect of God's love. In verse 4, "He careth for you" (*1 Peter 5:7*). In verse 7, God is our Redeemer. Verse 6 reminds us that our minds cannot envisage the breadth of his love. This verse is often omitted, yet it emphasises the breadth of God's love by pointing to the narrowness of man's: "But we make his love too narrow, By false limits of our own . . .". The invitation is thus (v.8) to come nearer Jesus, with simple trust in his love and in his word.

Throughout the hymn, the love of Jesus is the contrast theme: kindness (vv.2 and 5)—even "kindness in His justice" (v.3); *wide* mercy (v.3); *plentiful* redemption (v.7).

47

STRENGTHEN FOR SERVICE, LORD, THE HANDS . . .

"The very God of peace sanctify you wholly"
(*1 Thessalonians 5:23*)

---

1 Strengthen for service, Lord, the hands
    That holy things have taken;
Let ears that now have heard thy songs
    To clamour never waken.

2 Lord, may the tongues which 'Holy' sang
    Keep free from all deceiving;
The eyes which saw thy love be bright,
    Thy blessèd hope perceiving.

3 The feet that tread thy holy courts
    From light do thou not banish;
The bodies by thy Body fed
    With thy new life replenish.

This hymn is ascribed to Ephraim the Syrian (*c.* 306–373). It is thus one of the earliest hymns in any hymn book. However, its current use is still further east, hence the ascription "Liturgy of Malabar" in several hymnals.

This version of the hymn is by C. W. Humphreys (1841–1921), adapted by P. Dearmer. It is based on a prose translation of the prayer, published by J. M. Neale in 1859. Another version can be found in "Hymns Ancient & Modern Revised", by A. Fox: "Hands that have been handling holy things . . .". In that translation, successive verses refer to hands, ears, eyes, lips, feet, and bodies.

Of all the hymns in most hymn books, this must surely be the one with the most distant and the most unlikely source. The "Liturgy of Malabar" is the source: Malabar is neither in Europe nor the Middle East, but on the south-west coast of India. Here, Christian communities of fishermen have long existed, and the native church claims to have originated as a result of the missionary journey of St. Thomas to India in the 1st century. There is no written evidence to support this, but archaeologists have shown that there was considerable trade between the Near East and India at that time. Certainly, the Christian church in this part of India predates the coming of European missionaries. This hymn is a useful reminder that Christianity is not solely a European religion, and it never has been. Some hymn books print the first line in the original language, though in our script: "Hayyel Maran 'idhe daphshat".

The hymn is a prayer, the original of which is found in the 5th-century Nestorian Rite, which is used by the churches in Malabar. It is spoken by the deacon while the people are receiving communion. It is very simple, and yet very profound. Following the communion service, the thought moves on to serving the Lord outside the Church, and asks first (v.1.1) for strength. Then (v.2), in the light of the holiness experienced in the service, we ask to be kept from deceit (v.2.2), and to be kept in the joy of hope. We ask for true light and life (v.3), in order to lead Christian lives in the coming days. The idea is as valid for days in a factory or office as it has been for days of fishing in the Bay of Bengal.

Hundreds of other profound hymns must await translation from this and other Christian churches.

STRONG SON OF GOD, IMMORTAL LOVE

Alfred, Lord Tennyson (1809–1892)

"Now faith is the substance of things hoped for,
the evidence of things not seen"
(*Hebrews 11:1*)

---

1 Strong Son of God, immortal Love,
    Whom we, that have not seen
      Thy face,
    By faith, and faith alone, embrace,
Believing where we cannot prove;

2 Thou wilt not leave us in the dust:
    Thou madest man, he knows not
      why;
    He thinks he was not made to die;
And Thou hast made him: Thou art just.

3 Thou seemest human and divine,
    The highest, holiest manhood,
      Thou:
    Our wills are ours, we know not
      how;
Our wills are ours, to make them Thine.

4 Our little systems have their day;
    They have their day and cease to
      be:
    They are but broken lights of Thee,
And Thou, O Lord, art more than they.

5 We have but faith: we cannot know;
    For knowledge is of things we see;
    And yet we trust it comes from
      Thee,
    A beam in darkness: let it grow.

6 Let knowledge grow from more to
      more,
    But more of reverence in us dwell;
    That mind and soul, according
      well,
May make one music as before,

7 But vaster. We are fools and slight;
    We mock Thee when we do not
      fear:
    But help Thy foolish ones to bear;
Help Thy vain worlds to bear Thy light.

Alfred, Lord Tennyson, was born in 1809. He was the third son of the rector of Somersby, Lincolnshire. He was educated at the local grammar school in Louth, and at Trinity College, Cambridge. In 1850 he became Poet Laureate, and his poems are widely read and studied.

Tennyson never wrote a hymn. These verses are taken from the eleven verses that form the Prologue to his long poem "In Memoriam". This was published in 1850, and written in memory of his close friend Arthur Hallam, who but for his early death would have become Tennyson's brother-in-law. There are various versions in different hymn books, ranging from four verses to seven—while "Songs of Praise" has made two hymns from the verses. The author once said, "A good hymn is the most difficult thing in the world to write."

Most Long Metre hymns rhyme as couplets *aabb*, or in alternate lines *abab*; the *abba* rhymes of this hymn add to its distinctiveness.

This hymn contains profound ideas, and the meaning of several phrases is not immediately obvious. The first phrase, "Strong Son of God", must refer both to *Luke 2:40* ("the child [Jesus] grew and waxed strong in spirit. . . .") and to *Psalm 89:8* ("O Lord, who is a strong Lord like unto thee?"). After that, the whole of verse 1 is a subordinate clause, and the main sentence continues in verse 2. The theme of the whole hymn is *faith*. It is only through faith that we can come to the Son of God (v.1.3) because proof is impossible—as the writer to the Epistle to the Hebrews recognised (*Hebrews 11:1*). The rest of the hymn explores how faith is interlinked with feelings.

Verse 2 of both the poem and the hymn is printed as part of the same sentence as verse 1. But verse 2 of the poem has been omitted, and verse 2 of the hymn (opposite) is really a separate sentence. Originally it formed verse 3 of the poem. The sudden change of theme is explained by reading the original verse 2:

> Thine are these orbs of light and shade;
> Thou madest life in man and brute;
> Thou madest Death; and lo, thy foot
> Is on the skull which thou hast made.

The emphasis on the Son of God as Creator in this omitted verse is perhaps the chief ground of faith, leading also to reverence and humility, but sustaining hope beyond death. Thus the poet can make the confident assertion (v.2.1), "Thou wilt not leave us in the dust".

The grounds for this assertion are threefold: our belief that God made us (v.2.2); our feeling that life must have a purpose (v.2.3); and our belief that God is just (v.2.4).

Verse 3 explores the puzzle of man's will: we have a mind of our own. While we cannot know how this can be (v.3.3), we can indeed discover a reason: we are able to decide to make our wills "Thine" (v.3.4). Our wills can do many other things, such as create great systems, which, in the light of eternity, are merely little and ephemeral (v.4.1−2). Even the greatest and best are only "broken lights" of God.

Thus—in verses omitted from some hymn books—we return to faith (v.5.1). We believe faith comes from God (v.5.3) and thus we pray for faith to grow (v.5.4). "For by grace are ye saved through faith; and that not of yourselves: it is the gift of God" (*Ephesians 2:8*). The prayer widens (v.6.1−2) to ask for knowledge and reverence to grow too: "The fear of the Lord is the beginning of wisdom" (*Proverbs 1:7*); "If any of you lack wisdom, let him ask of God . . ." (*James 1:5*). This unity of mind and soul, creating "one music; but vaster" (v.6.3−4; v.7.1) is a concept that needs to be central to one's whole life. The hymn is thus a true prayer of faith.

THE DAY IS PAST AND OVER

"It is thou, Lord, only, that makest me dwell in safety"
(Psalm 4:8)

1 The day is past and over;
   All thanks, O Lord, to thee;
I pray thee that offenceless
   The hours of dark may be:
O Jesu, keep me in thy sight,
And guard me through the coming night.

2 The joys of day are over;
   I lift my heart to thee,
And call on thee that sinless
   The hours of dark may be:
O Jesu, make their darkness light,
And guard me through the coming night.

3 The toils of day are over;
   I raise the hymn to thee,
And ask that free from peril
   The hours of dark may be:
O Jesu, keep me in thy sight,
And guard me through the coming night.

4 Be thou my soul's preserver,
   O God! for thou dost know
How many are the perils
   Through which I have to go:
O Lord and Saviour, hear my call,
And guard and save me from them all.

Ancient hymns were not only found in Latin churches: the Greek churches also had a rich collection of hymns, relatively few of which are known in English. This hymn is taken from the late evening service of the Orthodox Church. It dates from the 6th or 7th century, when most of England was pagan. The authorship is uncertain. The hymn did not reach England until it was translated by J. M. Neale. He published it in a small-circulation journal "The Ecclesiastic and Theologian" in 1853, and then in his "Hymns of the Eastern Church" in 1862.

The coming of night must have been much more terrifying 1300 years ago than it is today: with few lights and rudimentary government and communications, there were very real dangers. But now, as then, our worries often come to the fore at dusk, and this hymn speaks as much to 20th-century man as to men of the 6th century. Thus the first 3 verses conclude with an identical prayer for Christ's presence and protection. Doubtless the words of the Psalms were in the mind of the author: "I will both lay me down in peace and sleep: for thou, Lord, only makest me dwell in safety" (*Psalm 4:8*), and "I laid me down and slept; I awaked; for the Lord sustained me" (*Psalm 3:5*).

In each verse of the hymn, before the prayer, comes thankfulness for the day: for the day itself (v.1), for its joys (v.2) and for its work (v.3) — a helpful way of thinking back over any day.

Evening is a time for reflection that looks beyond the immediate future, so the final verse prays for God's protection from future perils, known only to Him. "The Lord shall preserve thy going out and thy coming in from this time forth, and even for evermore" (*Psalm 121:8*).

THE GOD OF ABRAHAM PRAISE
Thomas Olivers (1725–1799)
"My praise shall be continually of Thee"
(Psalm 71:6)

1 The God of Abraham praise
   Who reigns enthroned above,
Ancient of everlasting days,
   And God of Love:
Jehovah, Great I AM,
   By earth and Heav'n confest;
We bow and bless the Sacred Name
   For ever blest.

2 The God of Abraham praise,
   At Whose supreme command
From earth we rise, and seek the joys
   At His right Hand:
We all on earth forsake,
   Its wisdom, fame, and power;
And Him our only Portion make,
   Our Shield and Tower.

3 Though nature's strength decay,
   And earth and hell withstand,
To Canaan's bounds we urge our way
   At His command.
The watery deep we pass,   ·
   With Jesus in our view;
And through the howling wilderness
   Our way pursue.

4 The goodly land we see,
   With peace and plenty blest;
A land of sacred liberty
   And endless rest;
There milk and honey flow,
   And oil and wine abound,
And trees of life for ever grow,
   With mercy crown'd.

5 There dwells the Lord, our King,
   The Lord our Righteousness,
Triumphant o'er the world of sin,
   The Prince of Peace:
On Sion's sacred height
   His Kingdom He maintains,
And glorious with His saints in light
   For ever reigns.

6 Before the great Three-One
   They all exulting stand,
And tell the wonders He hath done
   Through all their land:
The listening spheres attend,
   And swell the growing fame;
And sing, in songs which never end,
   The wondrous Name.

7 The God Who reigns on high
   The great Archangels sing:
And "Holy, Holy, Holy" cry,
   "Almighty King!
Who was, and is the same,
   And evermore shall be;
Jehovah, Father, Great I AM,
   We worship Thee."

8 The whole triumphant host
   Give thanks to God on high;
"Hail! Father, Son, and Holy Ghost,"
   They ever cry:
Hail! Abraham's God, and mine!
   (I join the heavenly lays),
All might and majesty are Thine,
   And endless praise.

I n contrast to so many wealthy "establishment" hymn-writers,
Thomas Olivers (1725–1799) was a poverty-stricken boy from
Tregynon, Montgomeryshire, orphaned at the age of 5, and with little
formal education. He became an apprentice to a shoemaker. He moved
to the "bright lights" of Bristol, where he heard George Whitefield preach
and was converted: the theme of the sermon was "Is not this a brand
plucked out of the fire?" Olivers became a travelling preacher for John
Wesley, and it is claimed that he travelled over 100,000 miles on
horseback in 25 years.
   This is the only hymn for which this author is now known. The
original had 12 verses, and almost every line had a Scripture reference
attached. Every one of the twelve verses is still in current use, but there

This is a unique and remarkable hymn in which several of the ideas, and the tune, are based on Jewish worship. Some parts are a paraphrase of the Hebrew Yigdal—a metrical version of the 13 articles of the Jewish creed. The Yigdal is thought to be mainly a 13th-century work, which is sung antiphonally at the close of the Sabbath-eve service.

Verse 1 emphasises the greatness and holiness of God—"Ancient of Everlasting Days" (*Daniel 7:9*) and the "Great I AM" (*Exodus 3:14*) for whom all time is present. In Judaism (and, incidentally, in Islam) this is *the* greatest and most vital concept. It is equally vital in Christianity, but this is easily forgotten because we find it easier to relate to Jesus as Man: this hymn redresses the balance.

Several verses speak of our pilgrimage towards Heaven. Jesus is in view (v.3.6), but the imagery is still thoroughly Old Testament. Heaven is the promised land of milk, honey, olive-oil and wine (v.4.5 & 6)—a description of farming in Israel. In this promised land is "The Lord our Righteousness" (v.5.2)—an Old Testament phrase from *Jeremiah 23:6*, used here in the New Testament context of Christ as our redeemer, who is ". . . made unto us wisdom, and righteousness and sanctification and redemption" (*1 Corinthians 1:30*).

The vision in this hymn of the greatness and holiness of God does not exclude ordinary mortals. One verse, often omitted from modern hymn books, includes the lines, "He calls a worm his friend; He calls himself my God". Thus the hymn can triumphantly return to the original theme at the end, but include the individual too: "Hail Abram's God *and mine*: I join the heavenly lays" (v.8.5, 6).

---

are many different selections of verses in different hymn books, and they also appear in varying sequences. Some hymn books use the singular (as in the original) and others the plural (as here). Olivers is reputed to have been inspired by the Hebrew Yigdal after hearing it sung at the Great Synagogue in Duke's Place, London. The name of the tune, "Leoni", is the name of the Jewish chorister at that service.

THE GOD OF LOVE MY SHEPHERD IS
George Herbert (1593–1633)

"The Lord is my shepherd: I shall not want"
(Psalm 23:1)

---

1 The God of love my Shepherd is,
    And he that doth me feed;
  While he is mine and I am his,
    What can I want or need?

2 He leads me to the tender grass,
    Where I both feed and rest;
  Then to the streams that gently pass:
    In both I have the best.

3 Or if I stray, he doth convert,
    And bring my mind in frame,
  And all this not for my desert,
    But for his holy name.

4 Yea, in death's shady black abode
    Well may I walk, not fear;
  For thou art with me, and thy rod
    To guide, thy staff to bear.

5 Surely thy sweet and wondrous love
    Shall measure all my days;
  And as it never shall remove
    So neither shall my praise.

George Herbert (1593–1633) lived only 39 years, but he is one of the very few men who is widely known both as a poet and as an author of hymns. In fact, he wrote poems only, and his poems were not used as hymns until a century after he died, when John Wesley adapted some of them. Thus, although he is one of the earliest English authors in our hymn books, George Herbert cannot be strictly regarded as a hymn-writer. His other well-known "hymns" are "King of Glory, King of Peace"; "Let all the world in every corner sing"; and "Teach me, my God and King".

He was born in Montgomery, in mid-Wales, and educated at Westminster and at Trinity College, Cambridge. He became a Fellow of Trinity College when only 22 years old. At the age of 32 he was ordained, and for the last 3 years of his life he was rector of Bemerton, in Wiltshire.

G eorge Herbert's hymn is not now the best-known hymn based on this most-loved Psalm, but it is one of the finest versions.

The role of the shepherd was more obvious both in Old Testament times and in the 17th century than it is today. Shepherds are less often seen now, and, when we do see one, he is likely to be in a Land Rover. Nevertheless, the concept of the shepherd's constant care is still part of popular culture—probably more because of knowledge of *Psalm 23* than through first-hand experience. So the linkage of God the Shepherd with love (v.1.1) as well as with food (v.1.2) is easily understood. "He is mine and I am his" (v.1.3) has its biblical origin in the Song of Songs, not the Psalms, but it aptly describes the relation both of Shepherd and sheep, and of Creator and believer. The rhetorical question, "What can I want or need?" (v.1.4), is answered in the rest of the psalm: God's care is manifest in many ways. The "grass" and "streams" of verse 2 suggest both material needs and spiritual food. In the original psalm, they stress the Shepherd's goodness, for both green grass and cool water are hard to come by in the semi-desert country of Israel. Verse 3 refers to our tendency to go astray, and is clearly based on the Prayer Book version of *Psalm 23:3*: "He shall convert my soul, and bring me forth in the paths of righteousness, for His name's sake". But the Authorised Version is not far from the poet's mind: "He restoreth my soul" is powerfully expressed in the line "And bring my mind in frame" (v.3.2).

In verse 4, both the hymn and the psalm suggest a quiet inner confidence, even in the most distressing outward circumstances. "The rod" is a guide, not a threat. The hymn ends with praise to God for his everlasting love: the answer to the question posed in verse 1 has been completed.

Almost every century offers a new hymn based on this psalm, and each version offers new insights. There are several hymns still in common use. The oldest is "The Lord's my Shepherd: I'll not want". Although it is usually attributed to the Scottish Psalter of 1650, its origins are in fact older than Herbert's poem, as it has been traced in part to W. Whittingham, who lived in the mid-16th century.

"The Lord my pasture shall prepare" by Joseph Addison (1712) is a much more elaborate poem, described by P. Dearmer as "a delightful example of the classically embroidered style of the Augustan age". Like Herbert, Addison also omits the complex fifth verse of the psalm from his poem: the most difficult verse to express in a hymn.

Sir H. W. Baker wrote "The King of Love my Shepherd is" for "Hymns Ancient and Modern" in 1868: it clearly owes some of its phrases to George Herbert's hymn. There are many other versions of *Psalm 23*. For example, Isaac Watts' "Psalms and Hymns" has three versions which are virtually unknown today: "My Shepherd is the living Lord" (Long Metre: 8888); "My Shepherd will supply my need" (Common Metre: 8686); and "The Lord my Shepherd is" (Short Metre: 6686).

T HE SPACIOUS FIRMAMENT ON HIGH
Joseph Addison (1672–1719)

"The heavens declare the glory of God; and the firmament sheweth his handywork. Day unto day uttereth speech, and night unto night sheweth knowledge. There is no speech nor language, where their voice is not heard."

(Psalm 19:1–3)

1 The spacious firmament on high,
With all the blue ethereal sky,
And spangled heavens, a shining frame,
Their great Original proclaim.
The unwearied sun from day to day
Does his Creator's power display,
And publishes to every land
The works of an almighty hand.

2 Soon as the evening shades prevail
The moon takes up the wondrous tale,
And nightly to the listening earth
Repeats the story of her birth;

Whilst all the stars that round her burn,
And all the planets in their turn,
Confirm the tidings, as they roll,
And spread the truth from pole to pole.

3 What though in solemn silence all
Move round the dark terrestrial ball;
What though nor real voice nor sound
Amid their radiant orbs be found;
In reason's ear they all rejoice,
And utter forth a glorious voice;
For ever singing as they shine,
'The hand that made us is Divine.'

T his hymn was first published in the weekly journal, "The Spectator", on August 23rd, 1712. The article was entitled "Faith & Devotion"; the theme was "the proper means of strengthening and confirming faith in the mind of man", and the text was the one printed above.

The article was signed simply "C", but it is unquestionably the work of Joseph Addison. He published four other hymns in "The Spectator", of which the most well known now are "When all thy mercies, O my God", and "The Lord my pasture shall prepare" (based on *Psalm 23*).

Joseph Addison was the son of an Anglican clergyman; at the time of his birth in 1672 his father was rector of Milston, near Avebury in Wilts., and he later became Dean of Lichfield. Joseph was educated at Charterhouse and at Oxford University. He wrote many essays on literary and political themes, as well as a play. He became Chief Secretary for Ireland: a major office of State at that time. He died in 1719 in London.

Only five hymns are printed with the Metrical Psalms and the Metrical Paraphrases "approved by the Church of Scotland, and appointed to be used in worship": two of them are by Addison, and the other three are virtually forgotten. There can be no better tribute to the quality of his hymns. This hymn could be criticised as not being distinctively Christian, for it could be accepted equally by Jew, Muslim, and Deist. But this is to misunderstand the purpose of the hymn, which is to focus, quite specifically, on God as Creator, and on us as individuals capable of an intelligent response. "Reason's ear" (v.3.5) is not just a reference to the 18th-century "Age of Reason", but also to our own thinking.

Man is blessed with intelligence, but his viewpoint is earthbound, and Addison writes about the heavens as seen by man. Thus the sun declares its Creator to each land in turn (v.1.7) by day, and the moon by night (v.2.1–4). Stars and planets are seen around the moon (v.2.5–8), although millions of miles apart, and all the heavenly bodies appear to "move round the dark terrestrial ball" (v.3.2). Addison is not intending to teach science through poetry, but to elucidate the joyful message of the heavenly bodies as seen by man. Thus sun, moon, stars and planets all proclaim their Creator: "The heavens declare the glory of God. . . . There is no speech nor language, where their voice is not heard." (*Psalm 19:1, 3*). Reason has led us to discover so much about these wonders of creation: we can join the praise of God, for both creation and the gift of reason.

THOU WHOSE ALMIGHTY WORD
John Marriott (1780–1825)

"God said, Let there be light: and there was light"
(*Genesis 1:3*)

1 Thou whose almighty Word
Chaos and darkness heard,
 And took their flight;
Hear us, we humbly pray,
And where the Gospel-day
Sheds not its glorious ray
 Let there be light!

2 Thou who didst come to bring
On thy redeeming wing
 Healing and sight,
Health to the sick in mind,
Sight to the inly blind,
Ah! now to all mankind
 Let there be light!

3 Spirit of truth and love,
Life-giving, holy Dove,
 Speed forth thy flight!
Move on the waters' face,
Bearing the lamp of grace,
And in earth's darkest place
 Let there be light!

4 Blessèd and holy Three,
Glorious Trinity,
 Wisdom, Love, Might;
Boundless as ocean tide
Rolling in fullest pride,
Through the world far and wide
 Let there be light!

John Marriott (1780–1825) was ordained after studying at Oxford, and spent most of his life serving in Devonshire. He did not allow publication of his hymns during his lifetime, and this hymn was first read—not sung—at a meeting of the London Missionary Society, shortly after his death.

Each verse of the hymn contains a world-wide message, yet nowhere is there any expression of over-confidence or superiority that mars some Victorian missionary hymns.

A hymn of four verses addressing in turn God the Father, God the Son, God the Holy Spirit, and finally God the Trinity, is a particularly appropriate form for Christian worship. This hymn is one of several which follow this format, but it is remarkable because it is based on the first three verses of the Bible.

To God the Creator we pray (v.1.4) that light should be shed everywhere (v.1.7). Our confidence in making this request rests on *Genesis 1:3*, when "chaos and darkness" (v.1.2) heard God's word and fled.

Verse 2, addressed to God the Son, also asks for light. In his first coming, Jesus brought healing and sight—both physically and spiritually—and now we pray to him for light to our minds (v.2.4, 5) as well as to our eyes. The author may well have been thinking of Jesus' application to himself of *Isaiah 61:1*. "He hath sent me to heal the brokenhearted, to preach deliverance to the captives, and recovering of sight to the blind, to set at liberty them that are bruised . . ." (*Luke 4:18*).

To the Holy Spirit we pray for light and grace (v.3.5). Just as in *Genesis 1:2*, where "the Spirit of God moved upon the face of the waters", so we ask the Spirit to move throughout the world (v.3.6).

The final verse concludes the prayer. We address the Trinity, source of divine Wisdom, Love and Might, and once again we pray for light.

We SAW THEE NOT . . .
J. H. Gurney (1802–1862)

"Blessed are they that have not seen, and yet have believed"
(*John 20:29*)

1 We saw thee not when thou didst come
   To this poor world of sin and death,
Nor e'er beheld thy cottage-home
   In that despised Nazareth;
But we believe thy footsteps trod
Its streets and plains, thou Son of God.

2 We did not see thee lifted high
   Amid that wild and savage crew,
Nor heard thy meek, imploring cry,
   'Forgive, they know not what they do';
Yet we believe the deed was done
Which shook the earth and veiled the
   sun.

3 We stood not by the empty tomb
   Where late thy sacred Body lay,
Nor sat within that upper room,
   Nor met thee in the open way;
But we believe that Angels said,
'Why seek the living with the dead?'

4 We did not mark the chosen few,
   When thou didst in the cloud ascend,
First lift to heaven their wondering view,
   Then to the earth all prostrate bend;
Yet we believe that mortal eyes
From that far mountain saw thee rise.

5 And now that thou dost reign on high,
   And thence thy waiting people bless,
No ray of glory from the sky
   Doth shine upon our wilderness;
But we believe thy faithful word,
And trust in our redeeming Lord.

John Hampden Gurney was born in London in 1802; his father was Sir John Gurney, a baron of the Court of the Exchequer. He studied law at Trinity College, Cambridge. Ordained at the age of 25, he was successively curate at Lutterworth, Leics., rector of St. Mary's, Bryanston Square, London, and a prebendary of St. Paul's Cathedral. For many years he helped with the work of the Religious Tract Society and the SPCK. He died in 1862. His best-known hymn is probably "Fair waved the golden corn, in Canaan's pleasant land", and he also wrote "Yes God is good: in earth and sky".

Of this hymn, Gurney himself wrote, "Successive alterations have left nothing of the original composition remaining but the first four words, and the repeated words". The idea for the hymn, having the first part of each verse negative and the second part positive, can be traced back to Anne Richter (née Rigby). In 1834, "We have not seen thy footsteps tread" appeared as a new, and anonymous, hymn in "Songs of the Valley", compiled by the Misses Carus Wilson. Gurney and others amended it in 1838, 1842 and 1851. The version above approximates to the 1851 edition, which was so changed from the original that Gurney put his own name to it. The story does not end here: in 1931 "Songs of Praise" published yet another new hymn (689) based on the same idea: "We saw thee not when, far away, Among the hills of Galilee . . ."

The first line of each verse at first seems unattractive—we sing hymns to affirm our faith, not to list negatives. Yet Gurney's structure for the whole hymn helps us both to praise God for his acts in history, and to explore the meaning of our own faith. Successive verses speak of the birth and childhood of Jesus (1), the Crucifixion (2), Resurrection (3), and Ascension (4) as facts of history. Each verse concludes with "But" or "Yet": an affirmation of faith in the supernatural purpose of these facts. Thus the hymn becomes a form of Creed. Indeed, the usual tune is "Credo" ("I believe"), and its change of key emphasises the contrast between what we accept as facts in the first 4 lines of verses 1–4, and what we believe by faith in the last couplet of each verse.

Verse 1 speaks of the first 30 years of Christ's life, from his birth to his ministry. Although we did not see him, yet there is historical evidence for the existence of the man Jesus. But we can never prove that this man who lived on earth was the Son of God—we accept it by faith, and have to affirm, individually and as a congregation, that we believe it.

The second verse moves to the Crucifixion. Historians may be satisfied that one of the many people crucified by the Romans was a man called Jesus, but by faith alone we believe he forgives sin (v.2.4) and has made Almighty God accessible (v.2.6—see *Matthew 27:51* and *Hebrews 10:19–22*). When we move to the Resurrection and Ascension (vv.3, 4) we move to events which can never be "proved". Yet the Christian faith does ask for intelligent acceptance of eye-witness reports: reason assists faith.

The final verse turns our attention to Christ's reign in heaven now, and his coming kingdom. Yet Gurney's picture of life on earth for the Christian now is utterly gloomy—only a wilderness experience. This is somewhat surprising from an author whose other hymns have a strong theme of gratitude for God's creation. This unsatisfactory ending surely needs amendment to praise God for his present blessings to us rather than to complain about his remoteness.

With every other hymn in this book, we comment on the words of the hymn as printed, but since there is a long history of amendments to this particular hymn we suggest a more positive final verse:

> And now that thou dost reign on high
> And thence thy faithful people bless,
> New mercies daily from the sky
> Lead us to praise with thankfulness
> For we believe Thy faithful Word,
> And trust in our redeeming Lord.

PRAISE GOD FROM WHOM ALL BLESSINGS FLOW

"Let the heaven and earth praise him"
(Psalm 69:34)

Thomas Ken (1637-1710) wrote hymns and prayers for his pupils at Winchester. His hymns seem calm and peaceful, but his life was far from peaceful: he was imprisoned in the Tower of London in 1688 and dismissed from his bishopric in 1691. This well-known doxology forms the conclusion both to his 'Morning Hymn' (Awake my soul, and with the sun...) and to his 'Evening Hymn' (Glory to thee, my God, this night...). The verse also forms an ideal conclusion to this book.

> Praise God, from whom all blessings flow,
> Praise Him, all creatures here below;
> Praise Him above, ye heavenly host,
> Praise Father, Son, and Holy Ghost.

AMEN